Fairburn Figures

THE FAIRBURN SYSTEM OF VISUAL REFERENCES

SET 1

Book 3 : MALE & FEMALE

SITUATION POSES & HANDS

I.S.B.N. 0-86250-030-3

Third Edition 1987

Printed in the UK by Penshurst Press Ltd.,
Tunbridge Wells.

Published by

GRAPHIC · BOOKS
INTERNATIONAL

Graphic Books International Ltd.
PO Box 349, Rue des Goddards,
Castel, Guernsey, Channel Islands (U.K.)
Tel: 0481 53125   Telex: 4191246   Fax (3&2a) 0481 57089

Full colour catalogue featuring hundreds of design related books available on request.

The Fairburn System is a unique and comprehensive source of figure reference invaluable to illustrators, creative studios, art schools and photographers.

Good reference is essential to artists, helps photographers to discuss with clients and to brief models.

This organised system saves time and money when you understand it and learn to get the best from it.

Contents

Introduction to "The Fairburn System of Visual References."

These unique books have been produced for one reason only : to provide a vast amount of hitherto unavailable figure reference material in a convenient manner. It is an essential piece of equipment for use by professional people and those in training who need to depict accurate graphic representations of human figures. Whilst every effort has been made to provide as much information as possible, it must be appreciated that any publication dealing with the action and poses of the human figure can never be definitive in the full sense of the word. The system of photography we have employed, however, allows the user, not only to obtain whole or part figure references, but to combine parts of such figures that have been photographed from a common viewpoint — thus increasing the reference material available by an enormous amount.

Because of the rapid change in fashions we have deliberately avoided using clothes which are not normal, everyday styles. All the basic types of garment are shown however and are easily adaptable.

Introduction à la Collection "The Fairburn System of Visual References."

Cette collection de livres sans égale a un seul but : fournir d'une manière pratique et facile à consulter une vaste somme de données informatives sur la figure humaine, qui n'était pas disponible précédemment. C'est un outil indispensable pour tous les professionnels et les étudiants qui veulent une représentation graphique précise de la figure humaine. Tous les efforts possibles ont été faits pour fournir le maximum de renseigne-ments; il faut néanmoins se rendre compte qu'aucune représentation de l' action et des poses de la figure humaine ne sera jamais complète ni absolue. Toutefois, le système de photographie que nous avons employé permet à l'usager non seulement de se procurer des références de figures entières ou partielles, mais encore de combiner des parties des figures qui ont été photographiées d'un point de vue commun : cela accroit énormé-ment le matériel de référence disponible.

La mode changeant rapidement, nous avons délibérément évité d'employer des vêtements qui ne sont pas normaux et courants. Toutefois, on peut trouver tous les types essentiels de vêtements; ils sont très facilement adaptables.

Satz: "The Fairburn System of Visual References."

Dieser einzigartige Satz Bücher ist nur zu einem Zweck herausgebracht worden : eine große Menge an bisher nicht verfügbaren Darstellungen der menschlichen Figur in praktischer Form. Es ist ein unerlä ßliches Hilfsmittel für alle im Beruf und in der Ausbildung, die präzise graphische Darstellungen des menschlichen Körpers anfertigen müssen. Einerseits sind in den Büchern so viel Informationen wie möglich gegeben, andererseits mu ß man sich darüber im klaren sein, da ß ein Buch über Bewegungen und Haltungen des menschlichen Körpers nie ganz erschöpfend sein kann. Die photographische Methode, die wir benutzt haben, ermöglicht es dem Benutzer, nicht nur die Gesamt- und Teildarstellungen einzeln zu benutzen, sondern Teile solcher Darstellungen, die unter einem gemeinsamen Gesichtspunkt photographiert worden sind, zu kombinieren, wodurch sich die Materialmenge ganz erheblich vergrö ßert.

Wegen der sehr häufigen Änderungen in der Mode haben wir mit Absicht keine Kleidungsstücke verwendet, die aus dem Rahmen des Üblichen und Alltäglichen herausfallen. Alle wichtigen Arten von Kleidungsstücken sind jedoch abgebildet, und sie lassen sich leicht abändern.

Introduccion al Juego "The Fairburn System of Visual References."

Este juego de libros verdadermente excepcional ha sido preparado por un solo motivo : el de proporcionar en forma conveniente una gran cantidad de material de referencia que hasta ahora no se podía obtener con facilidad. Es un equipo esencial para uso de profesionales, y para aquellos que están recibiendo un adiestramiento que necesita representar en forma gráfica y fidedigna la figura humana. Aunque se han hecho todos los esfuerzos posibles por proporcionar la máxima cantidad de información posible, debe tenerse en cuenta que cualquier publicación que se ocupe de los movimientos y posiciones de la figura humana no puede ser definitiva en el verdadero sentido de la palabra. Sin embargo el sistema de fotografia que hemos empleado permite al usuario no sólo el obtener referencias totales o parciales de la figura sino tambien el combinar partes de esas figuras que han sido fotografiadas desde un ángulo común, aumentando de esa forma de manera considerable el material de referencia.

Debido al cambio rápido de la Moda hemos evitado de manera deliberada el uso de ropas que no sean de un estilo normal y cotidiano. Pero de todos modos todos los tipos básicos de ropas pueden verse en la publicación y son fáciles de adaptar.

Figure drawing the professional way . . .

Like all the most useful commercial ideas, the Fairburn System of Visual References is distinguished by its simplicity.

For over a decade in over 100 countries the Fairburn System has provided a unique solution to a universal need for good reference material, essential to good drawing. By improving your reference material you can quickly improve your work. Research has found that the average illustrator/ artist wastes a considerable amount of time hunting for reference. How much is **your** time worth? There are two principal ways to increase your income, improve your work and increase your speed. The Fairburn System helps you to do both with a well-organised system of photographs of human figures and faces.

The complete 9 volume system contains over 25,000 photographic references. They come as three sets, so arranged that the pose or facial expression you may need is quickly available.

If you're an illustrator, visualiser, art director or anyone who needs to draw figures quickly and accurately, then you will immediately appreciate the value and potential of the system.

To make the most of these books always keep them to hand and familiarise yourself with the content sequence — this will help you to find the most suitable pose for any particular need with the minimum of delay.

For the majority of poses, several viewpoints have been provided as models were placed on a turntable and rotated past three cameras at low, medium and high angles and from eight positions — the result, 24 viewpoints. This 24 viewpoint sequence was used on the majority of photographs in the Fairburn System making it possible to create figures based on composite references from different parts of the system, e.g. the face, hairstyle, torso, legs, each coming from different picture references.

The books have been designed to open reasonably flat for positioning under enlarging devices so making copies for re-sizing and reference purposes is acceptable, but it must be made clear that under the terms of the publishers copyright, direct reproduction or publication of the images is not permitted.

The Fairburn System is without question the most comprehensive and widely used figure reference system available today but only comes into its own when used by illustrators who also "understand" the nature and construction of the human form. Therefore it is recommended that anyone lacking confidence in figure drawing should acquire a good reference book on human anatomy.

Used with skill, flair and imagination, combined with different illustration styles and techniques, the Fairburn System is an invaluable reference tool for any studio. A few examples of illustrations based on reference from this particular volume are shown on the next three pages. If you produce any illustration of which you are particularly proud, please send Graphic Books International a copy for possible use in future promotion literature — full credits will be given.

the complete FAIRBURN SYSTEM . . .

Set 1 · Figures and Hands
Includes 7,689 adult figure and hand pictures. Key poses are shown from 24 different angles to allow you to study the identical pose from all sides. One is bound to be just what you need.

Book 1 · Male Full Figure
Each page shows a different pose such as standing, sitting, walking, kneeling, lying etc. Since just one pose in each basic group would obviously not be sufficient we have shown several variations of that pose.

Book 2 · Female
The range of poses shown in this book is almost identical to Book 1. A wide variety of costume has been used on the models but care has been taken to use basic garments which will not go out of date too soon. Some of the poses, in order to increase the range of the book, have been photographed using nude models.

Book 3 · Poses and Hands
The first part of this book is filled with models involved in a specific activity where the complete situation is required to supply the necessary information. This includes such subjects as gardening, shopping, cleaning, dancing, do-it-yourself work, bathing and so on. The second part contains almost a thousand photographs of hands — again photographed in the system of 24 pictures per pose. Hands are shown in all the basic positions and also holding many implements and objects.

Set 2 · Faces and Heads
480 pages filled with 8,240 fantastic faces. Indexed by age, ethnic group and character type. Each head is photographed from 3 levels — 8 angles. Combine features to create your own character.

Book 1 · Males
This book shows all age groups from late teens to the very old, and many basic facial types — bearded, bald, handsome, ugly, thin, fat, meek, aggressive and so on. As full a range of expressions and emotions as possible are shown in each age and type group.

Book 2 · Females
This is the female version of Book 1. Again, all ages from late teens to the very old are shown together with a wide range of facial types and expressions.

Book 3 — Ethnic and Character Types
The first part illustrates many basic international types — broken down into five main groups: Oriental, Asian, African, Middle East/Mediterranean and South American. The second part features 'larger-than-life' characters such as the career woman, the military type, the pugilist and so on; There are also sections featuring such useful reference subjects as anatomical models of the skull and superficial muscles, male headwear, dramatic lighting effects on the face, the use of binoculars and telescope — all photographed to the basic system.

Set 3 · Children
Good photographic reference is essential in the difficult task of drawing children. Fairburn Set 3 contains 9,105 photographs of children of all ages and races.

Book 1 · Boys
Divided into five sections by age group: babies, young children, juniors, sub teens and teenagers. Each section comprises of several pages of faces followed by full figure poses, including lying, crawling, sitting, walking, running, lifting, stretching, jumping, pulling etc. Each again photographed from the 24 different angles.

Book 2 · Girls
This is a female version of Book 1. Again divided into five sections. Remember that when selecting a pose, particularly with young babies, unless they are in the nude, there is very little difference between sexes. Even in older groups, some boy and girl models can be interchanged with just a few strokes of your pencil.

Book 3 · Poses and Hands
Includes — Babies: breast feeding, bottle feeding, spoon feeding, bathing, nappy changing, dressing, sleeping, sitting on potty. Young children: Bathing, climbing, dressing, eating, playing, reading, sleeping, washing. Plus older children: Climbing, dressing, playing, reading, eating, fighting. Parent and child, family groups, children in groups, hands and feet, faces and dramatic lighting.

The following pages show drawings by various artists rendered entirely from Fairburn reference. The page number and actual size reproduction of the reference photo are included.

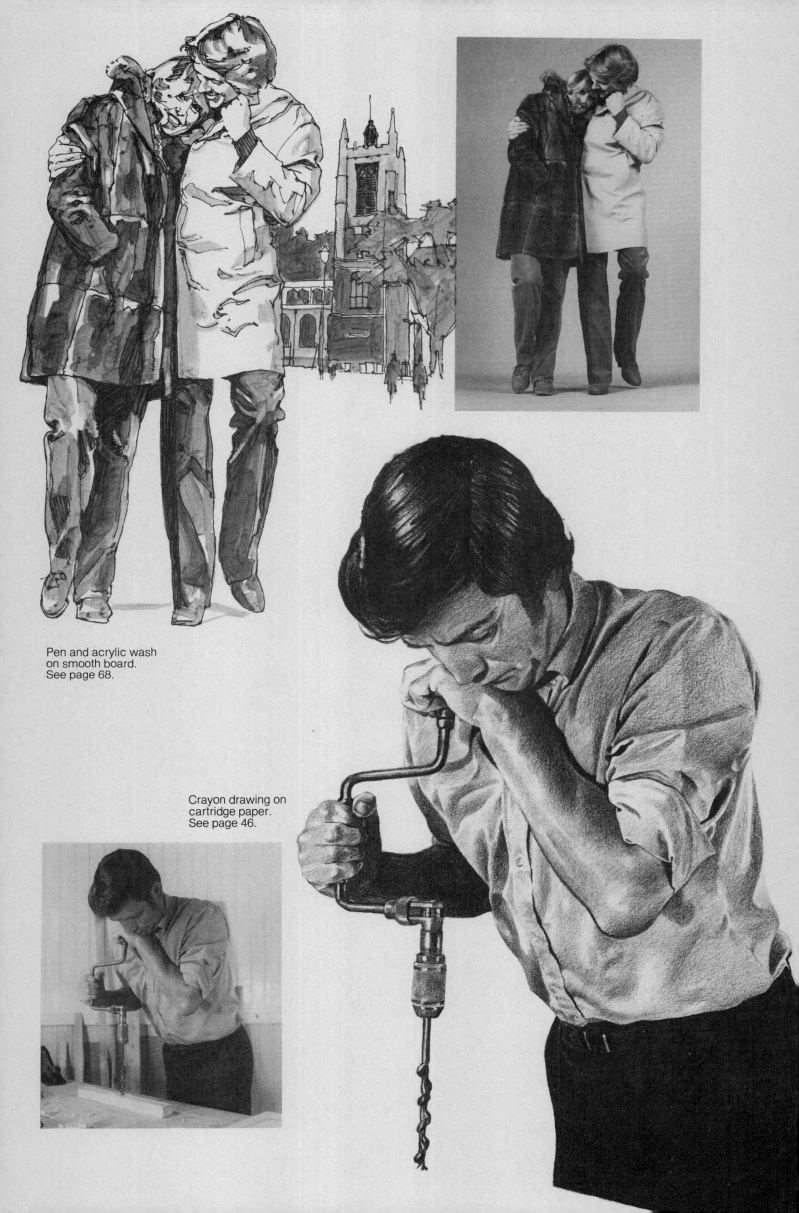

Pen and acrylic wash
on smooth board.
See page 68.

Crayon drawing on
cartridge paper.
See page 46.

Conté and watercolour wash on slightly textured board. See page 73.

Black and grey felt markers on layout paper. See page 56.

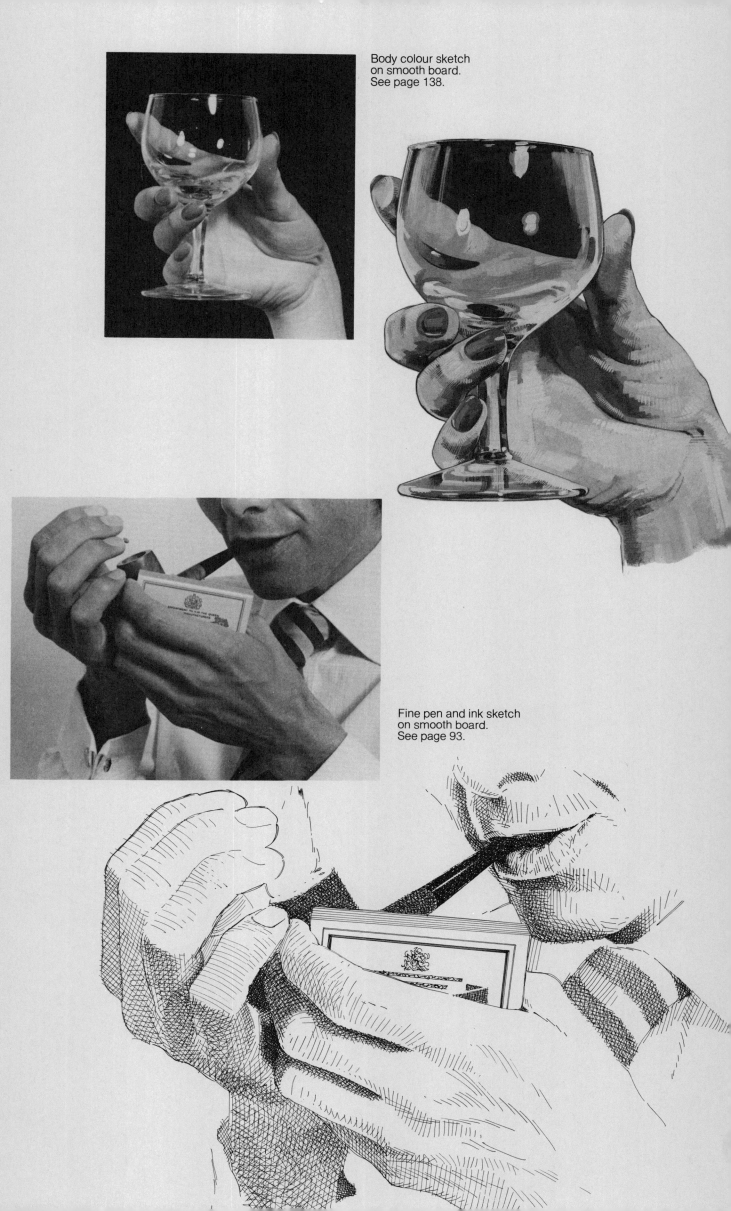

Body colour sketch
on smooth board.
See page 138.

Fine pen and ink sketch
on smooth board.
See page 93.

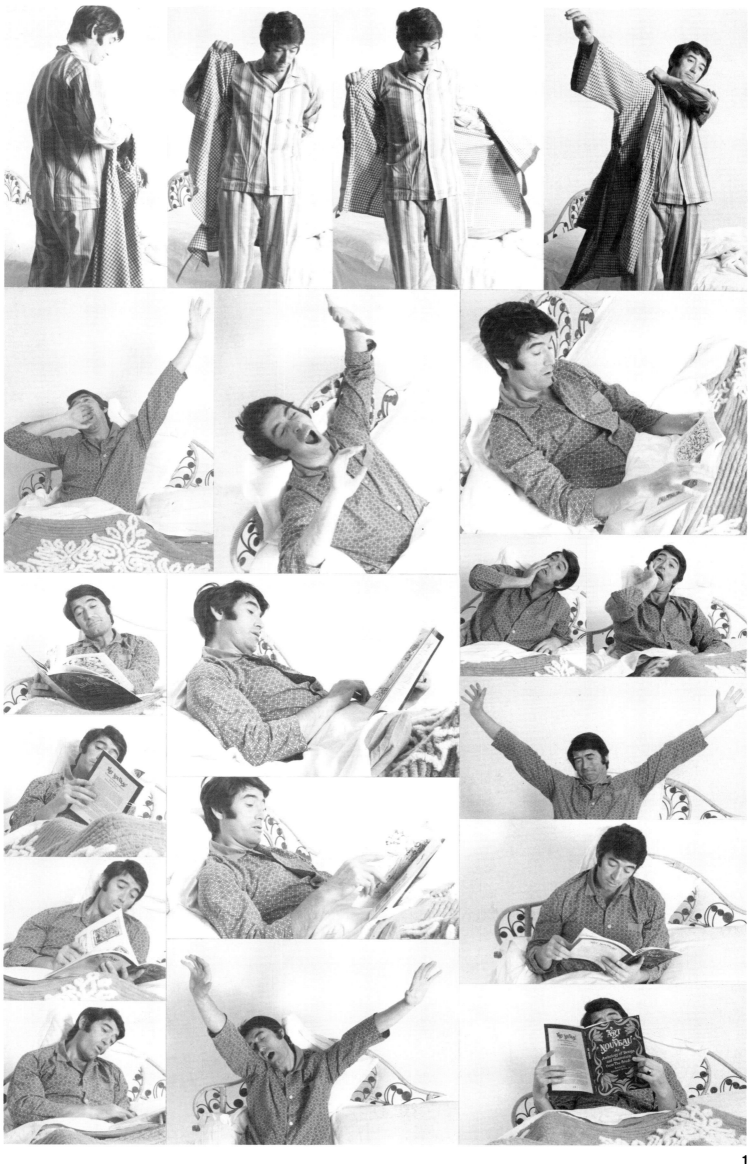

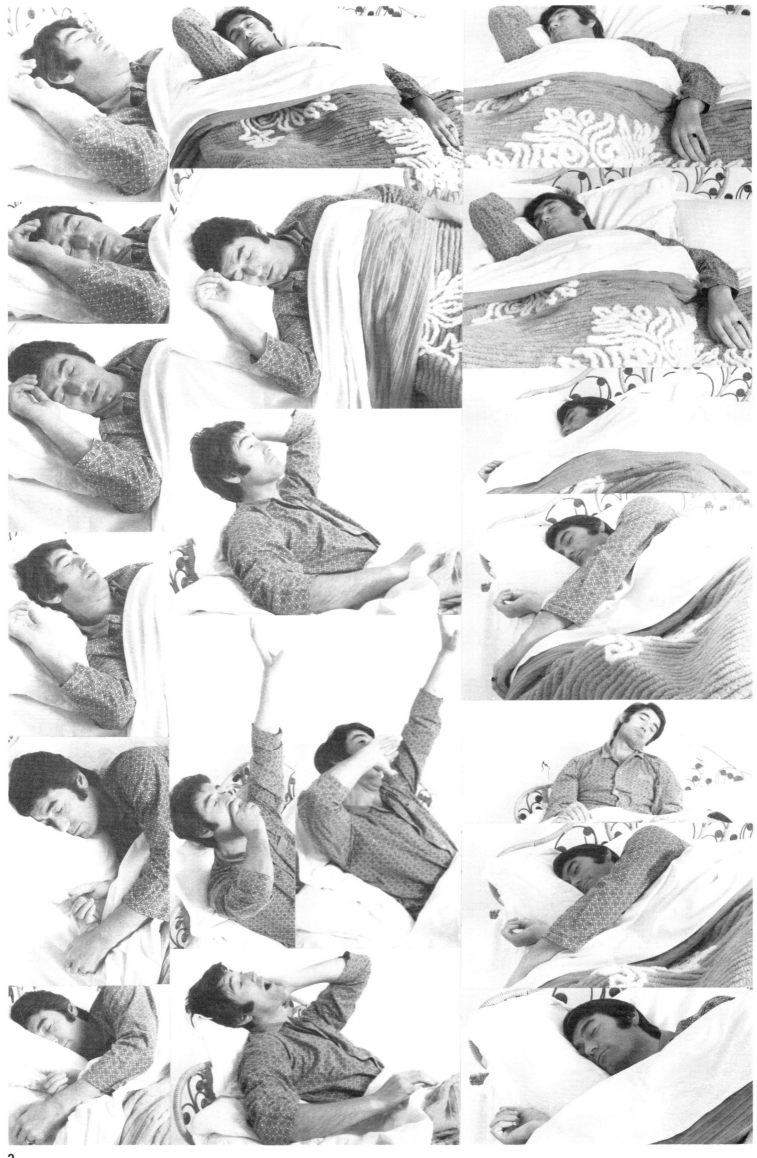

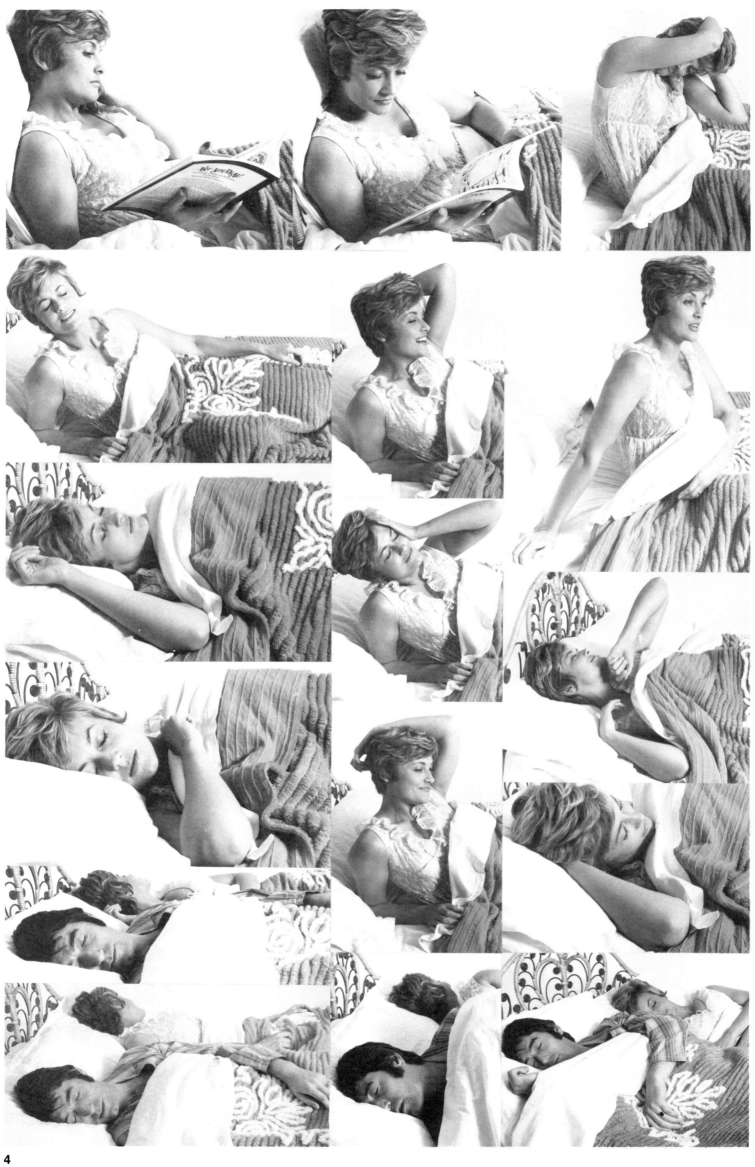

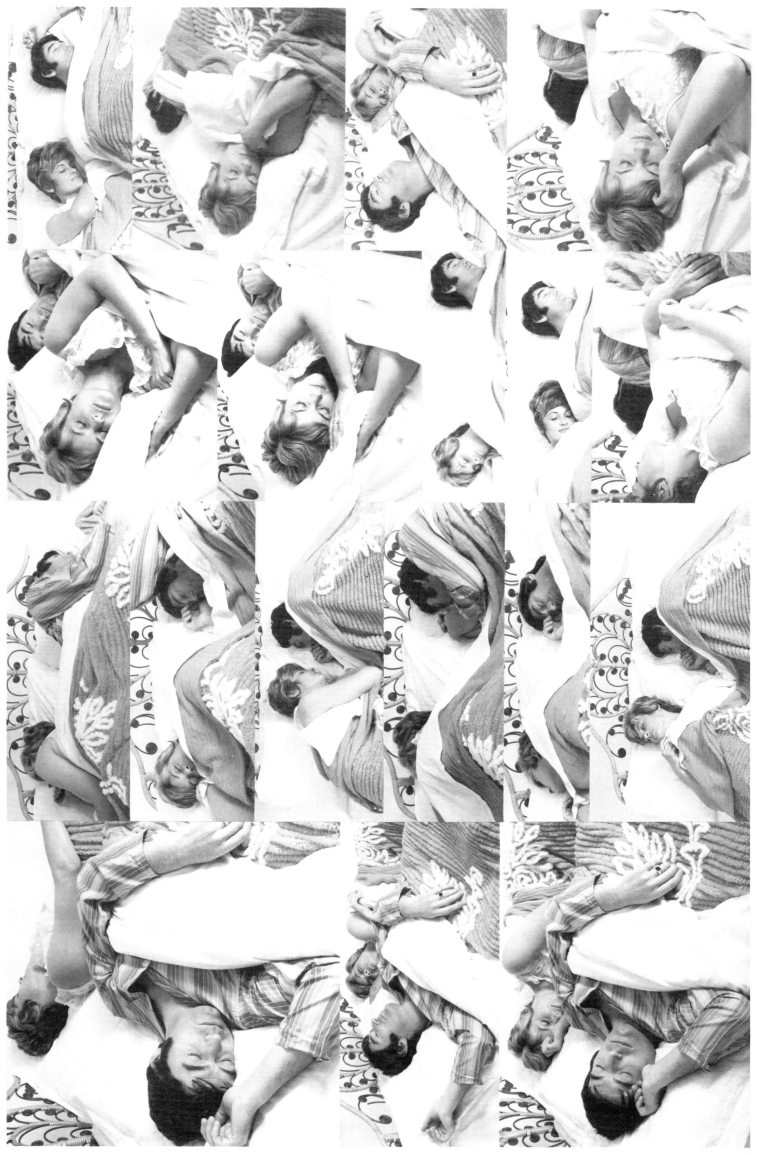

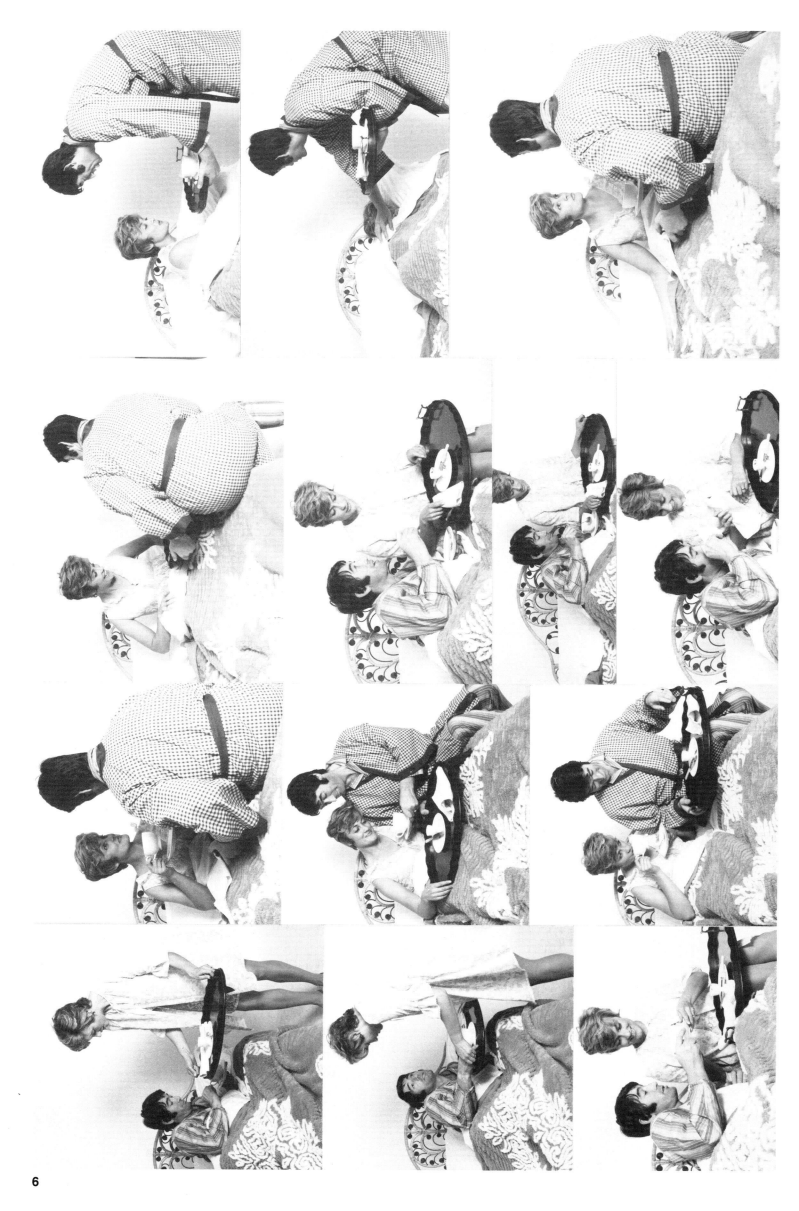

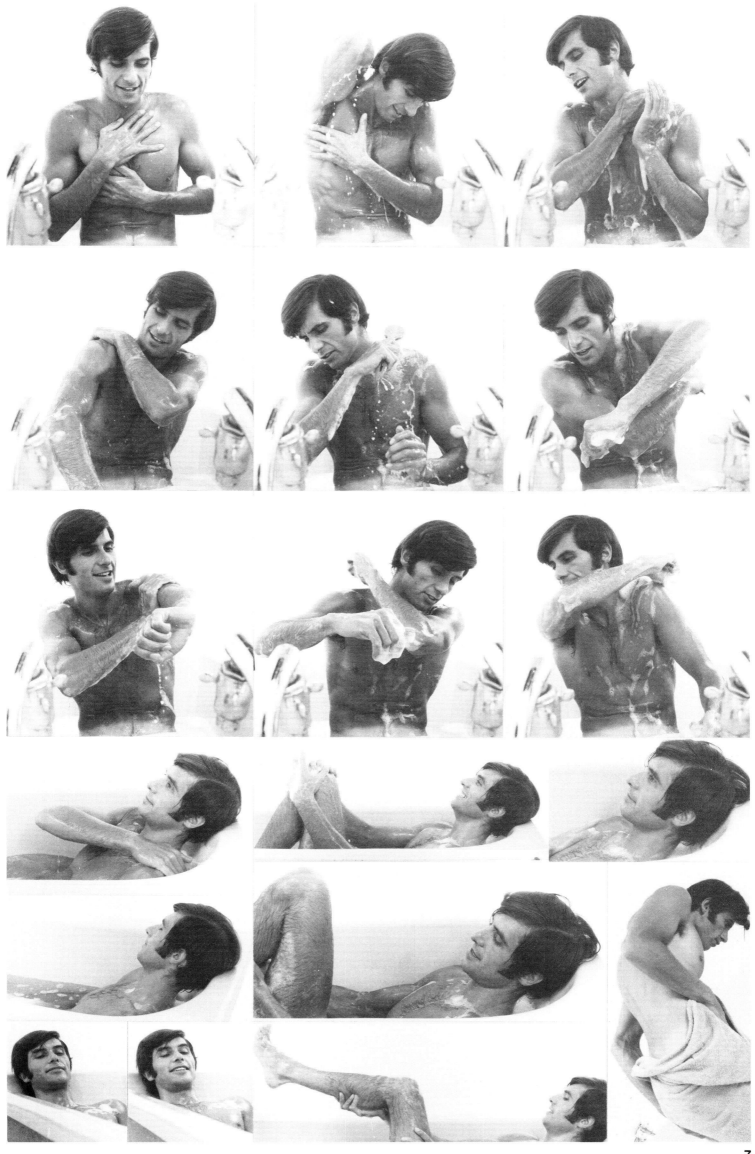

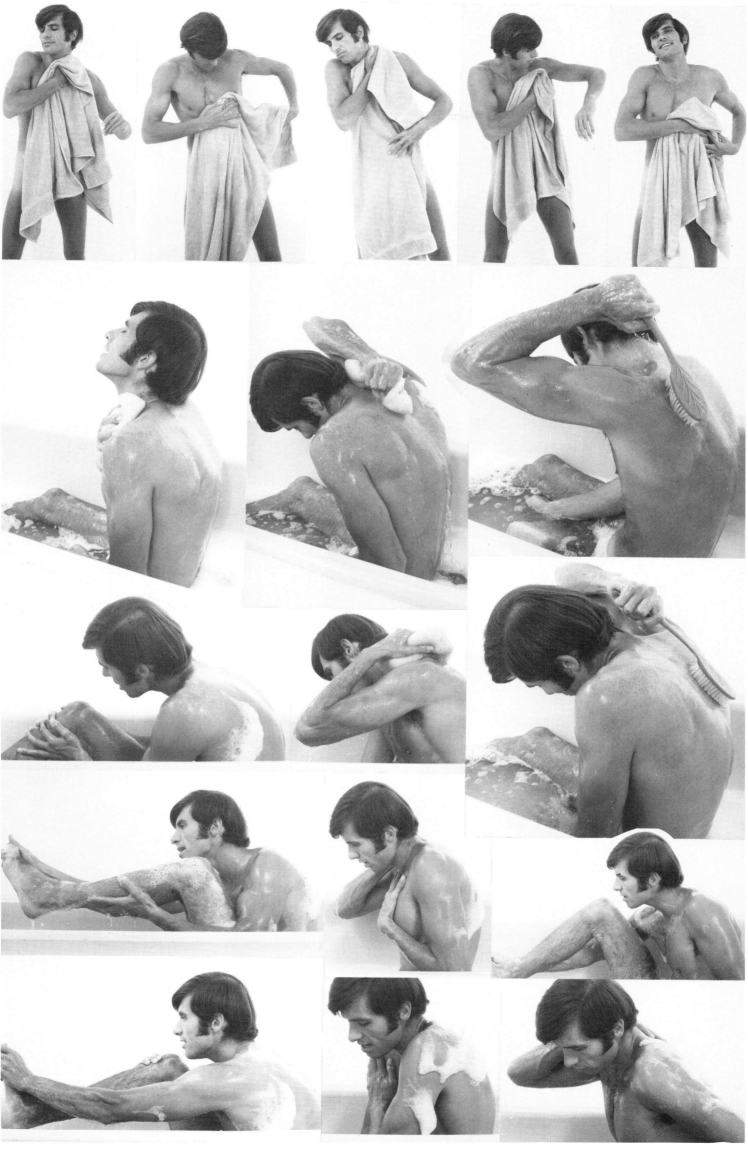

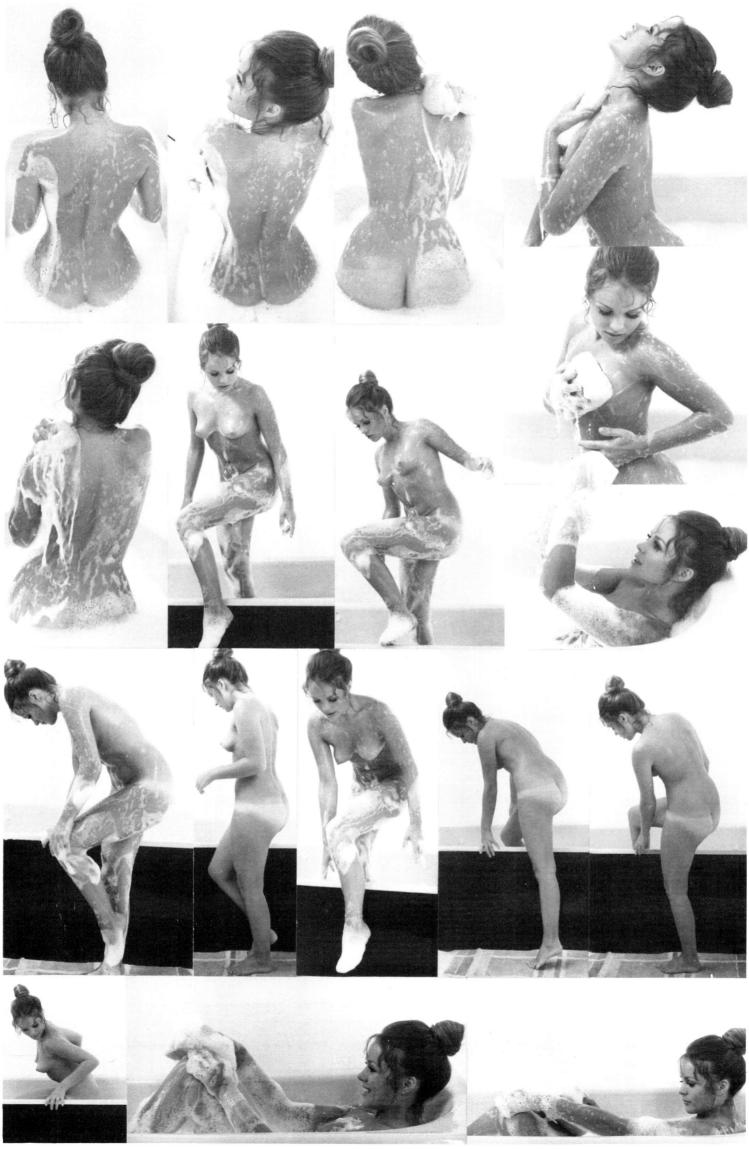

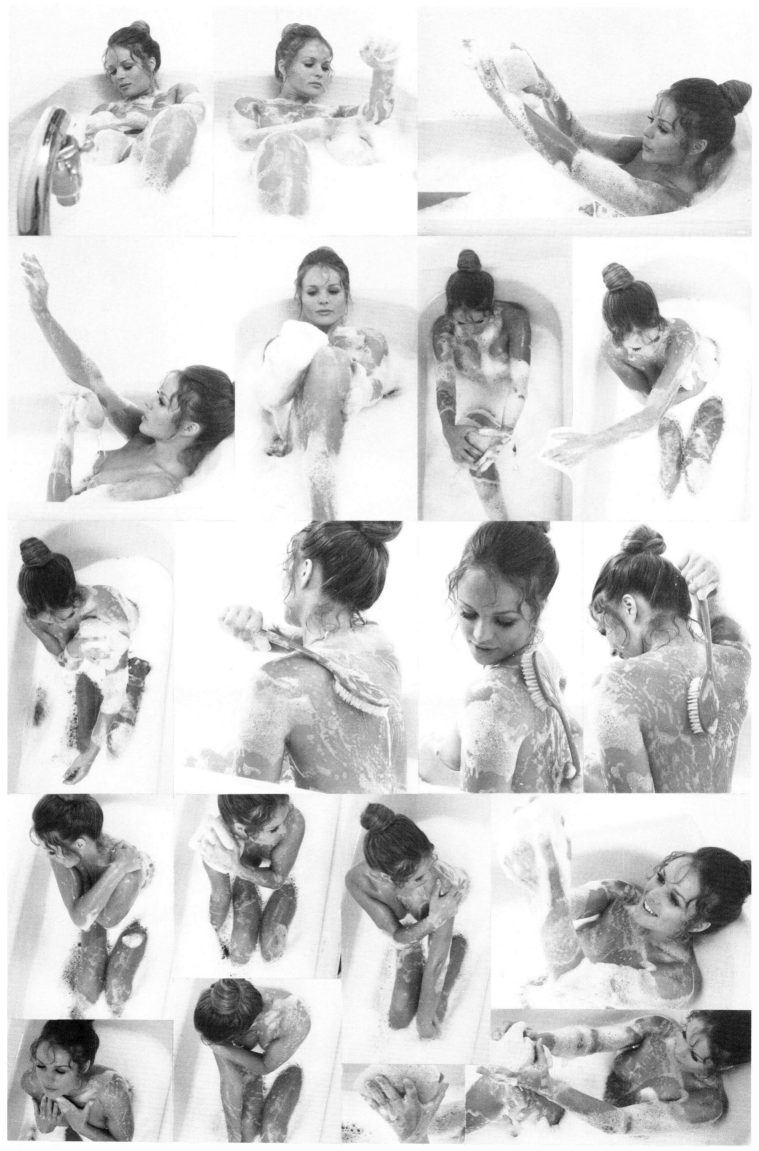

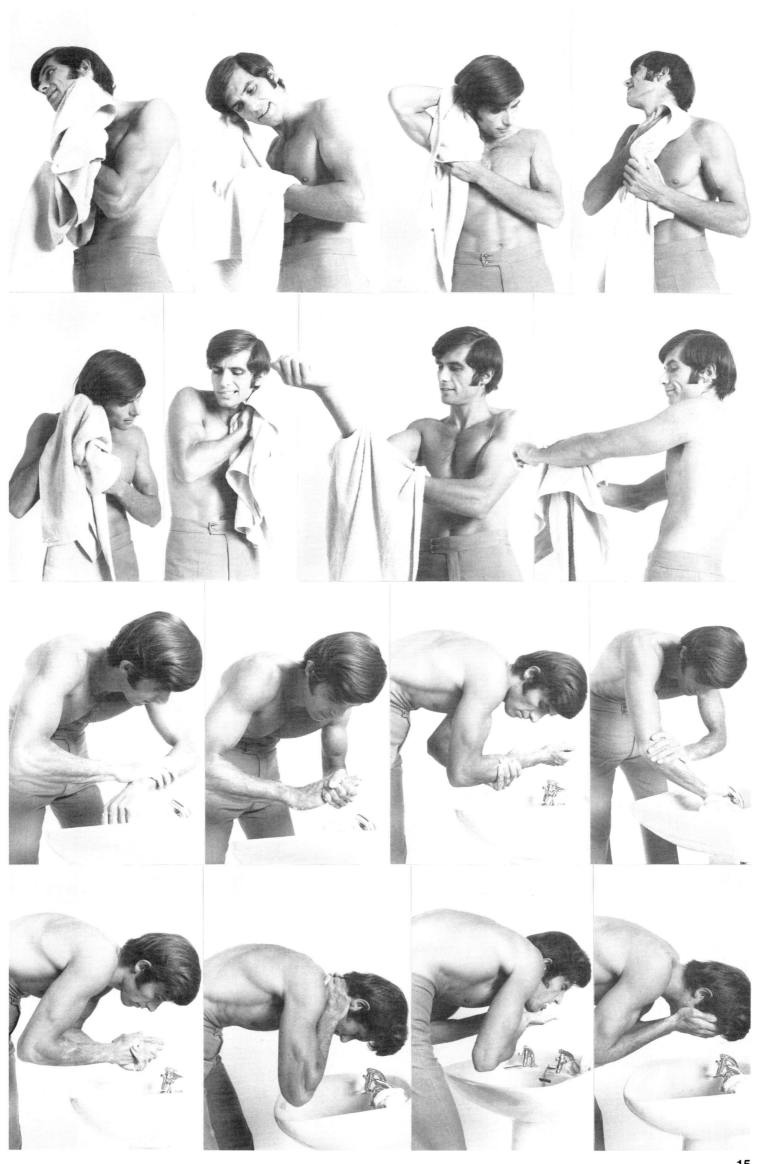

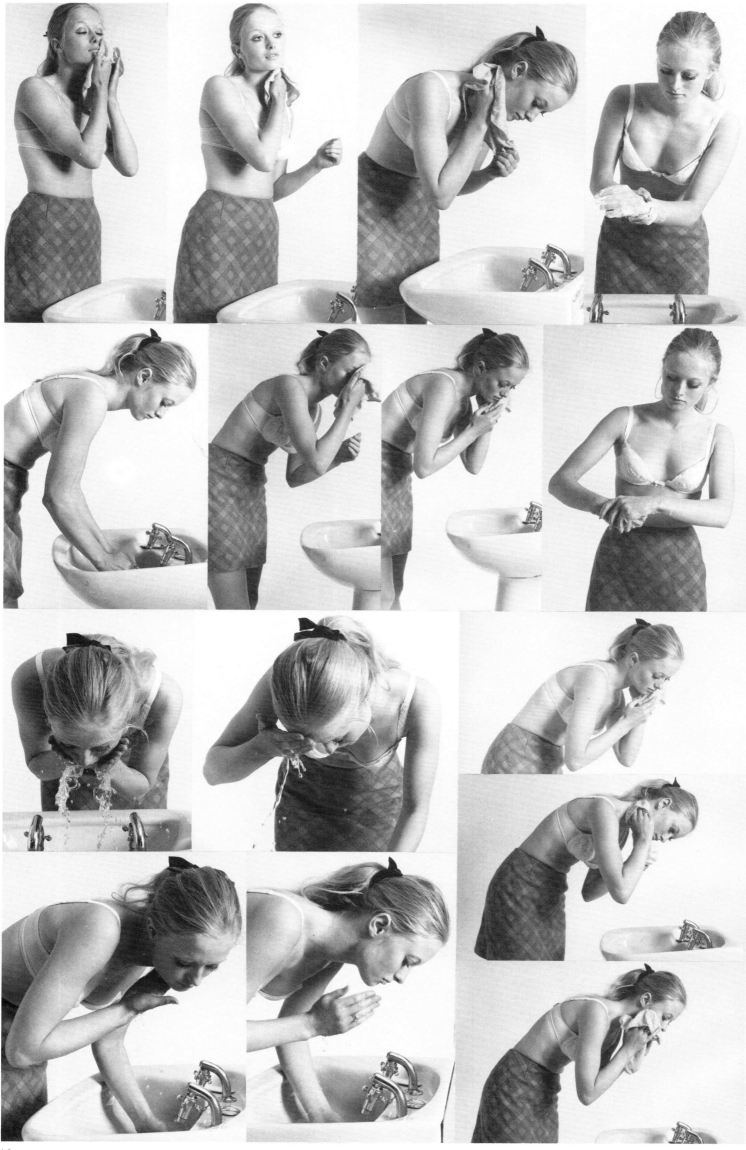

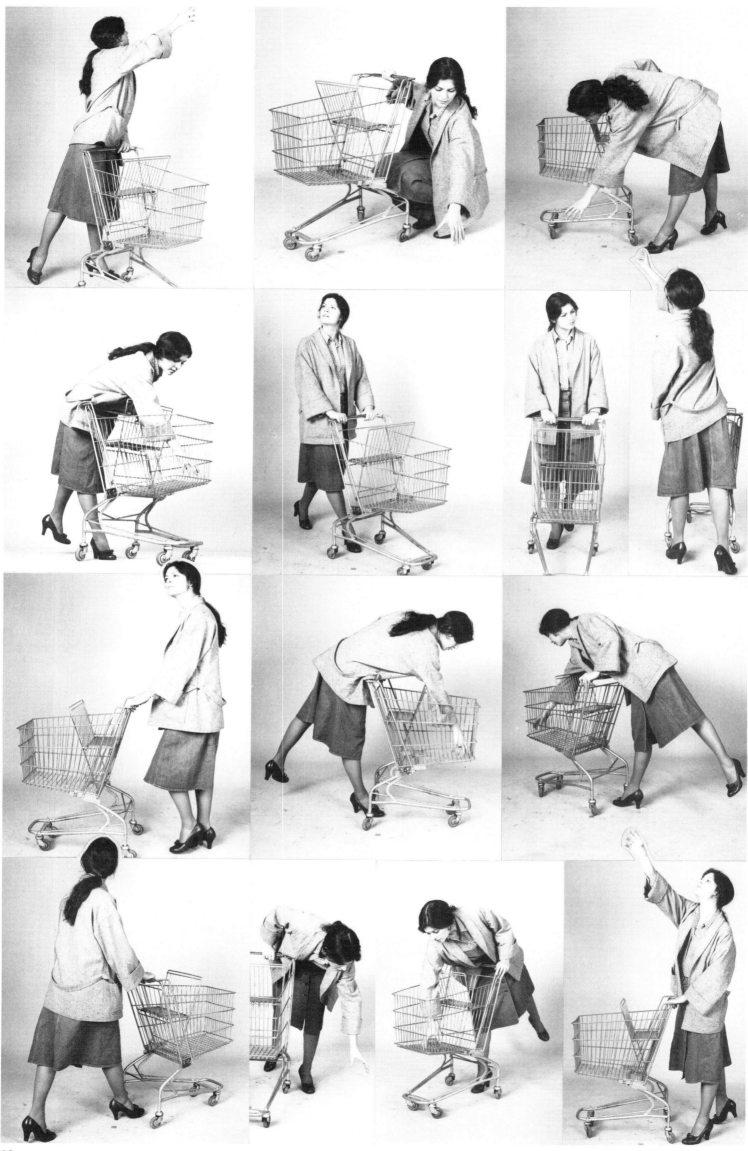

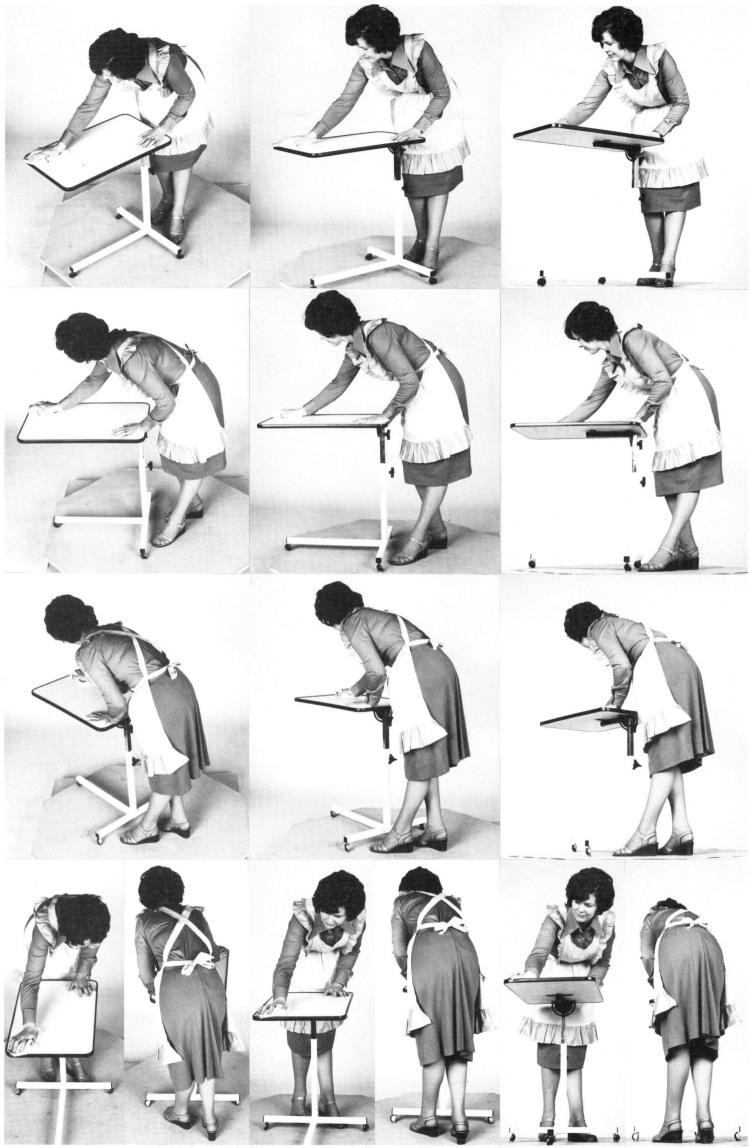

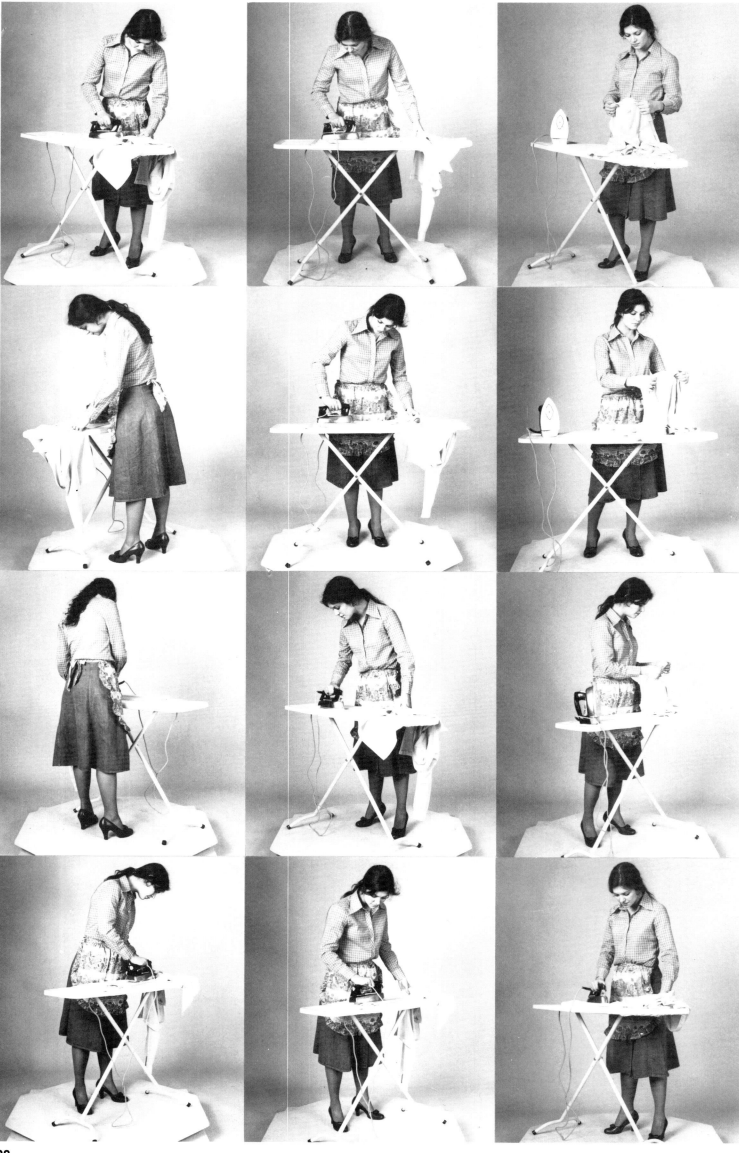

28

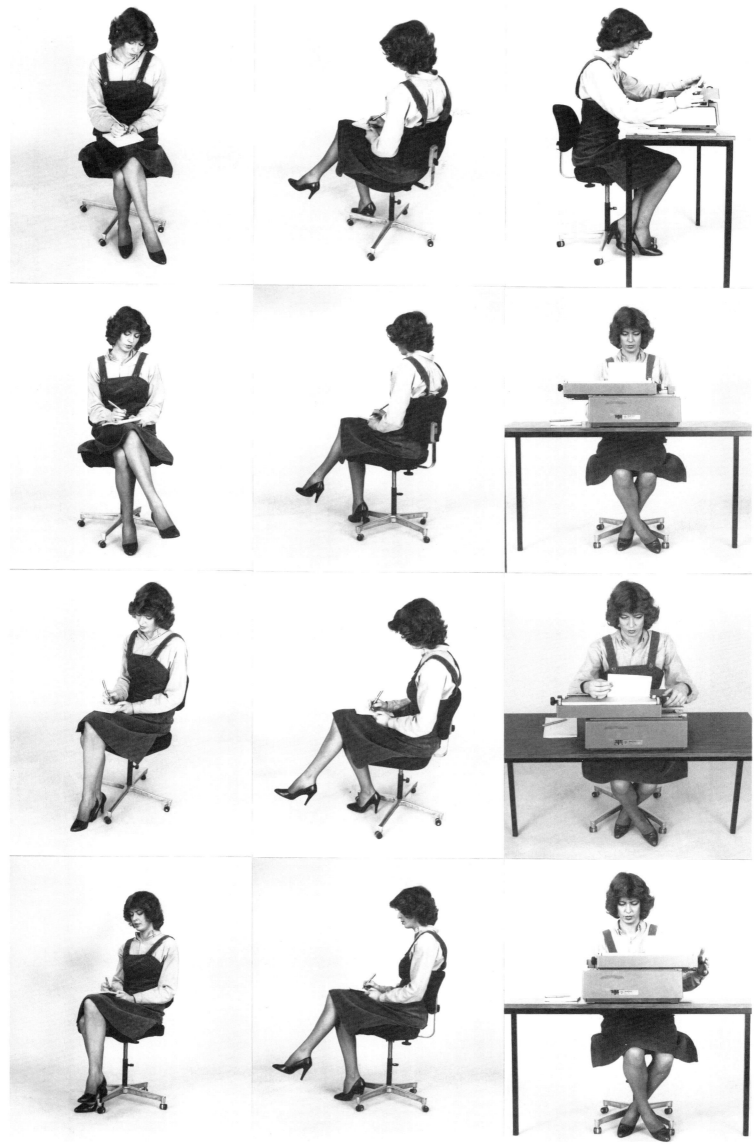

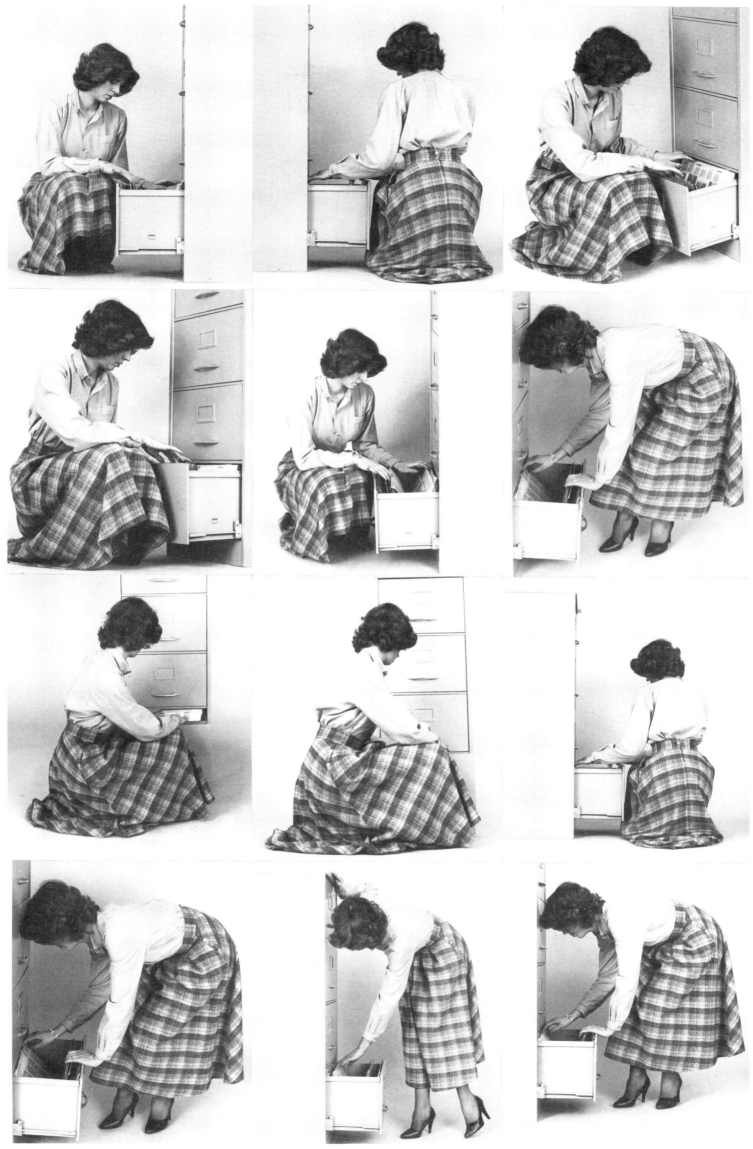

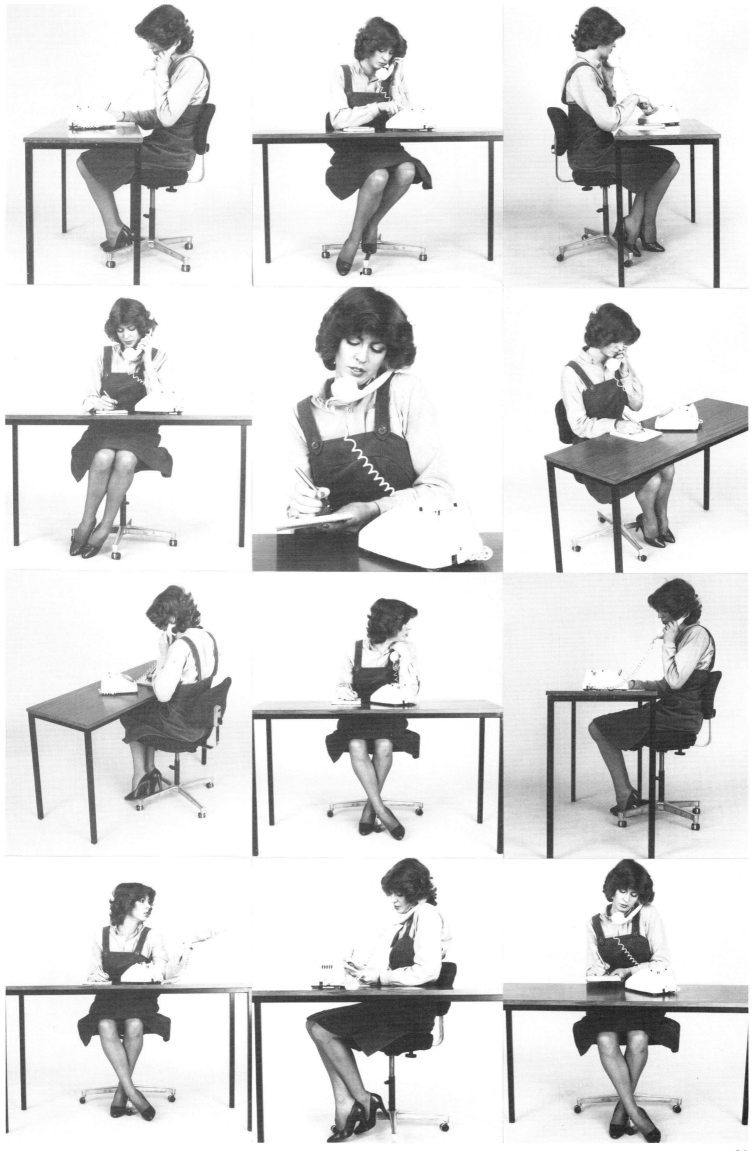

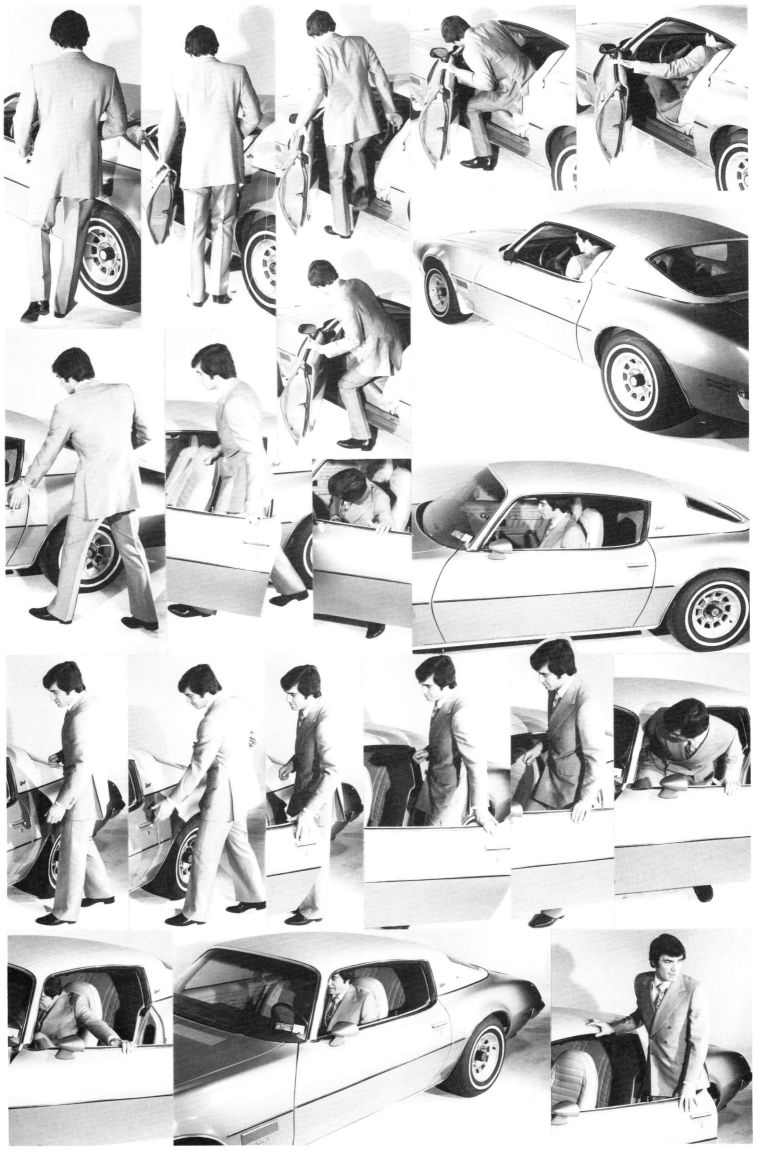

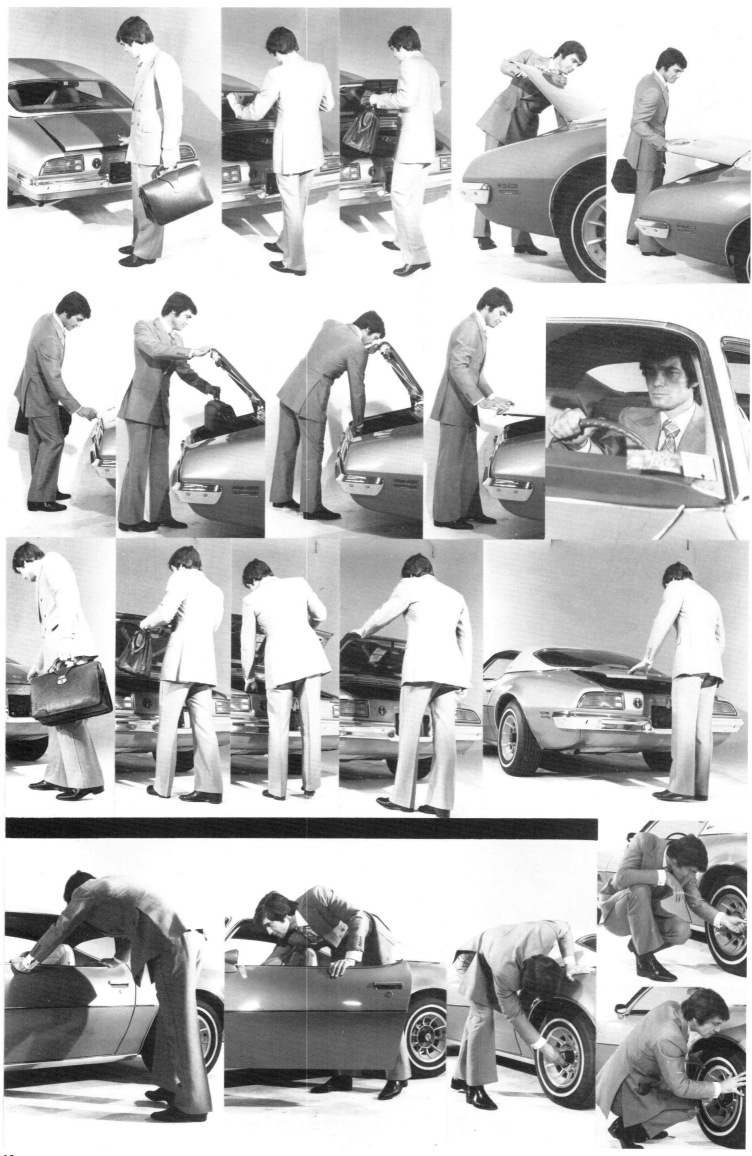

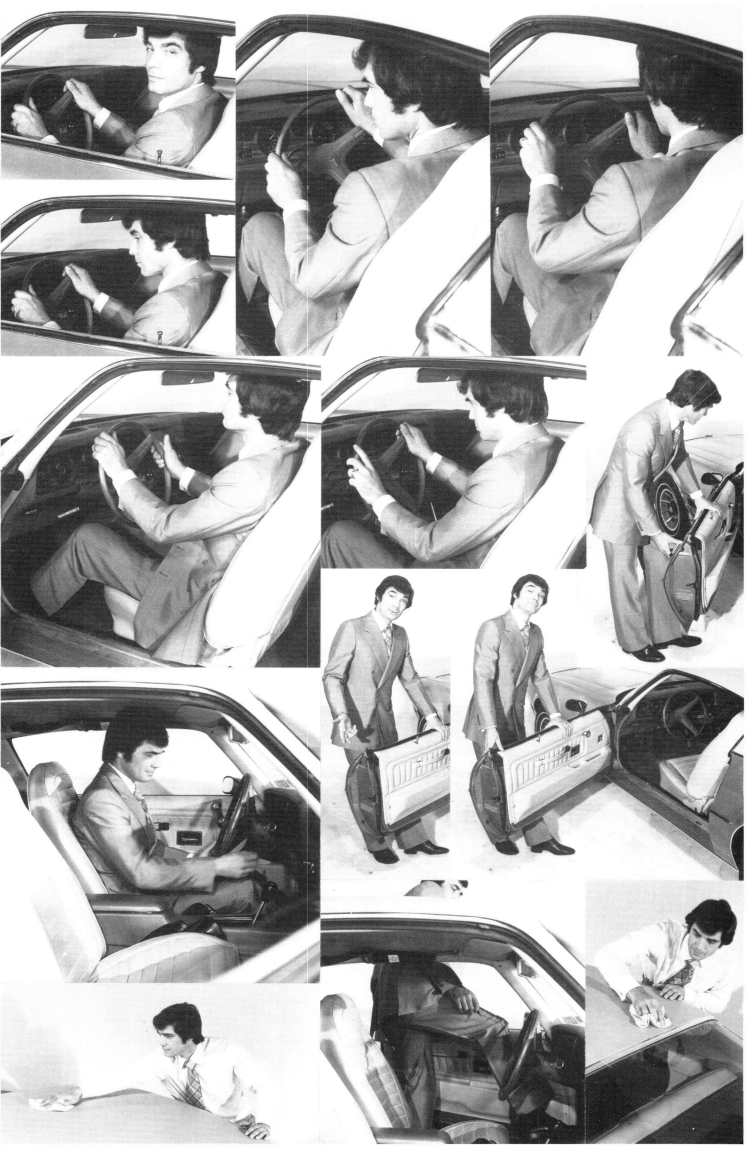

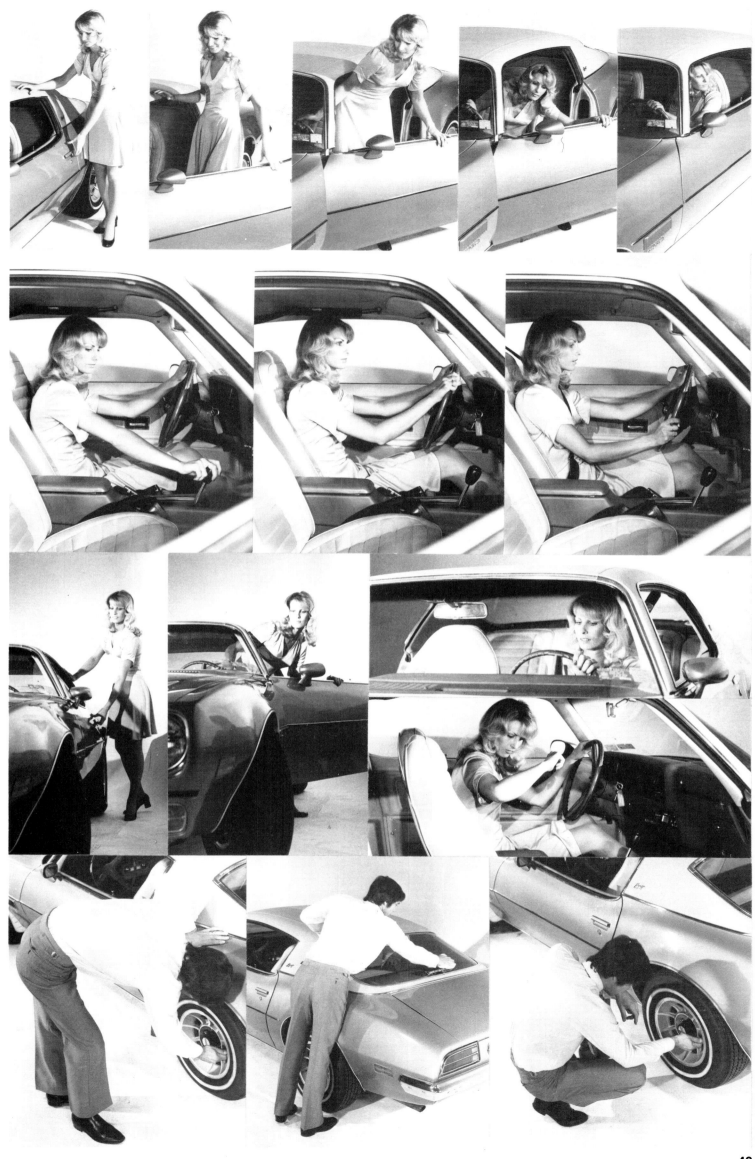

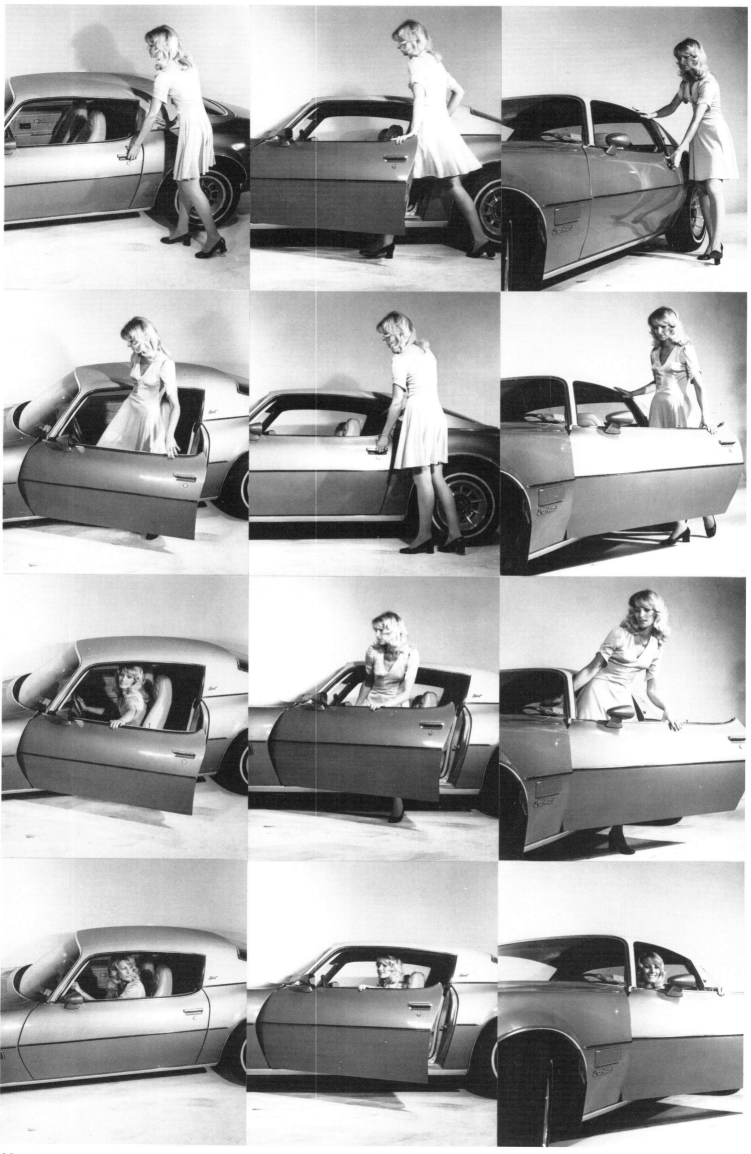

44

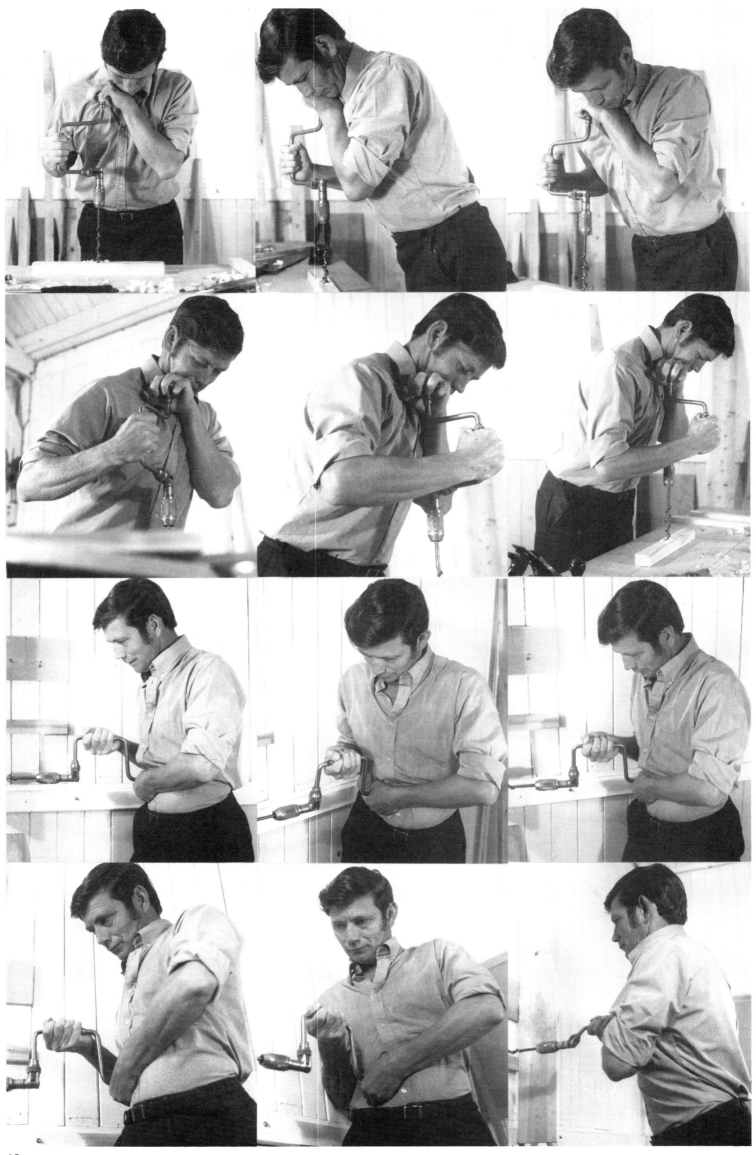

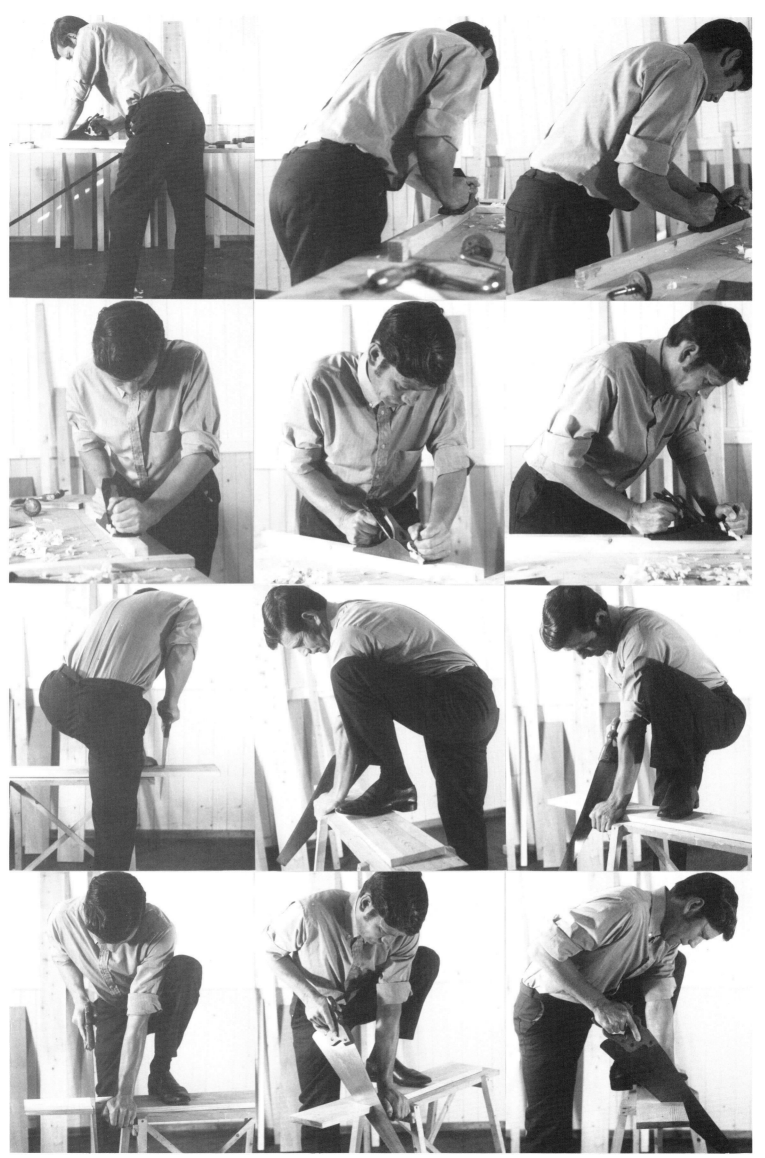

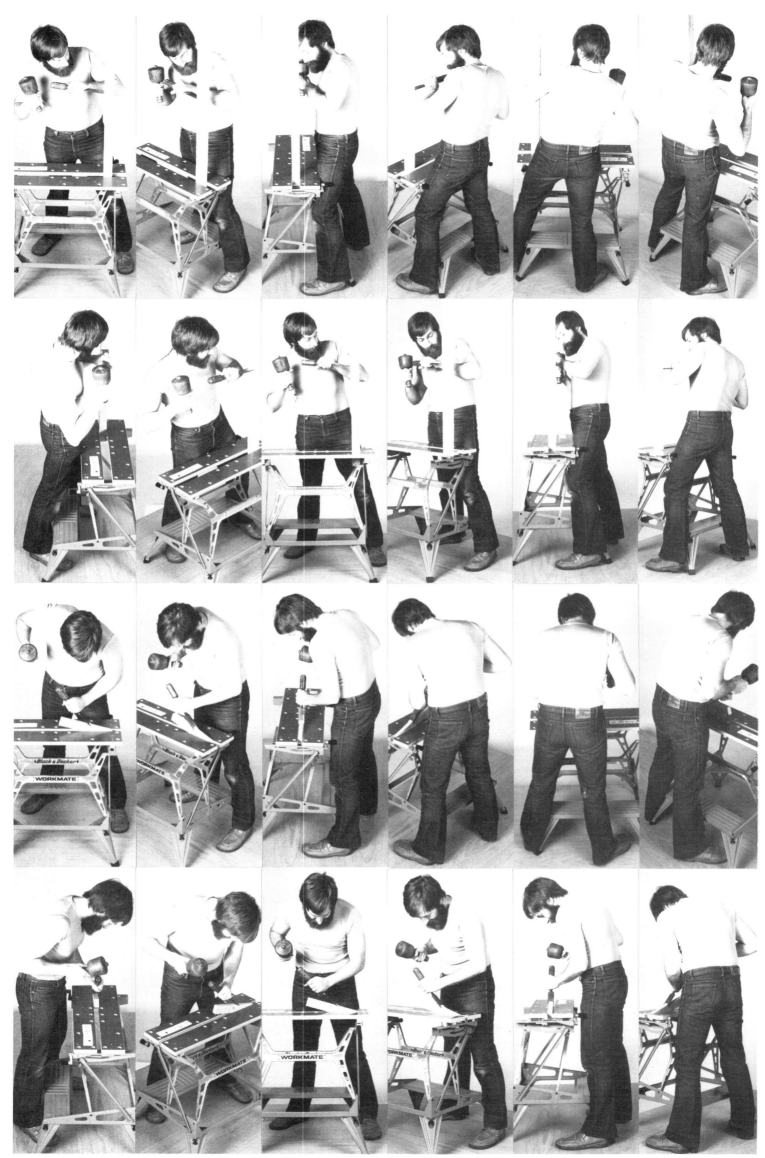

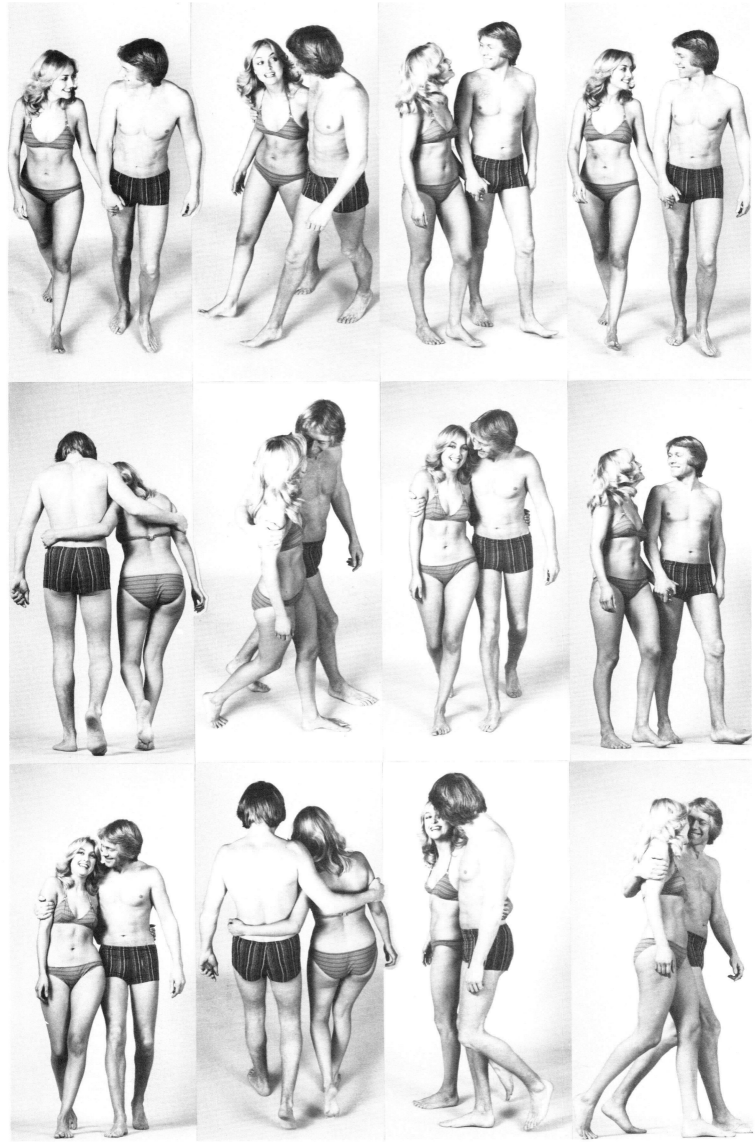

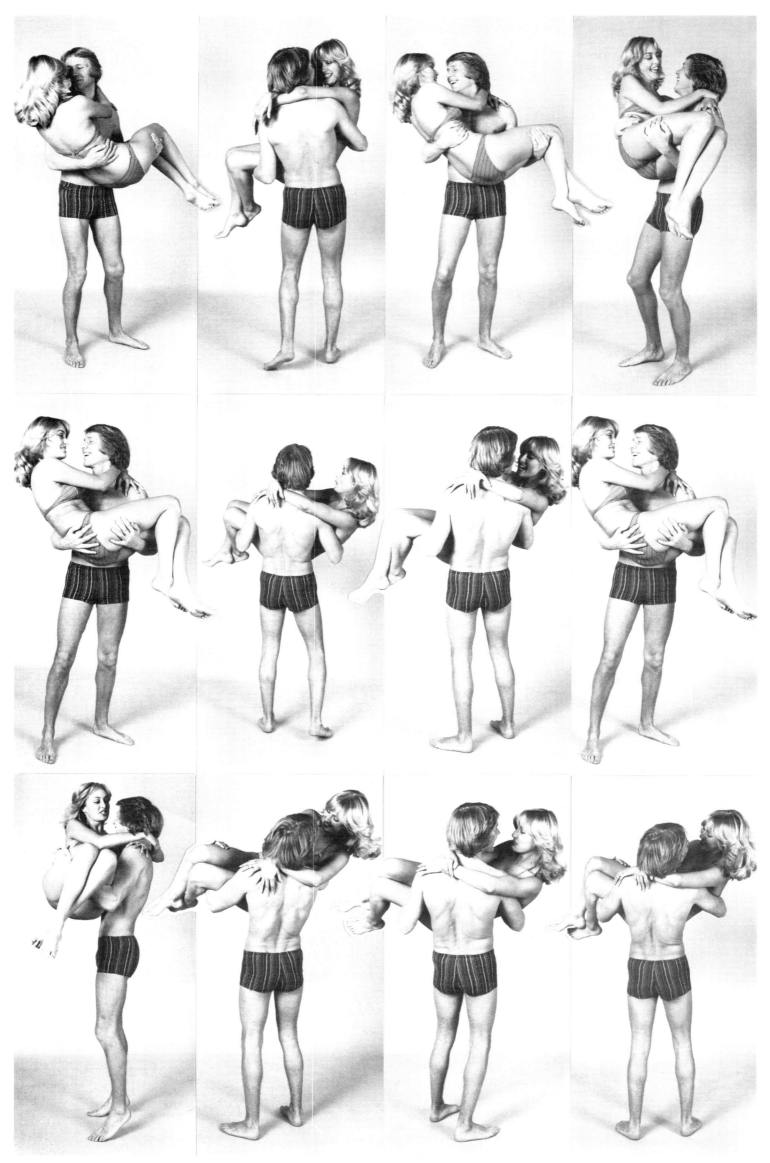

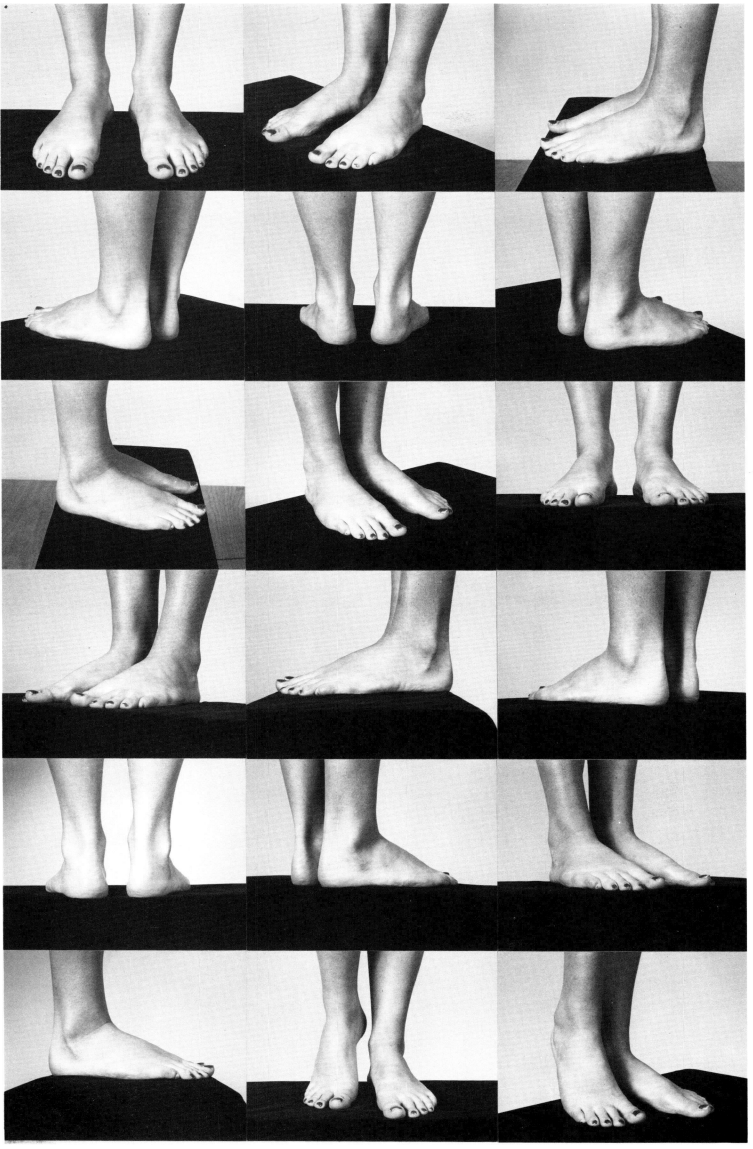

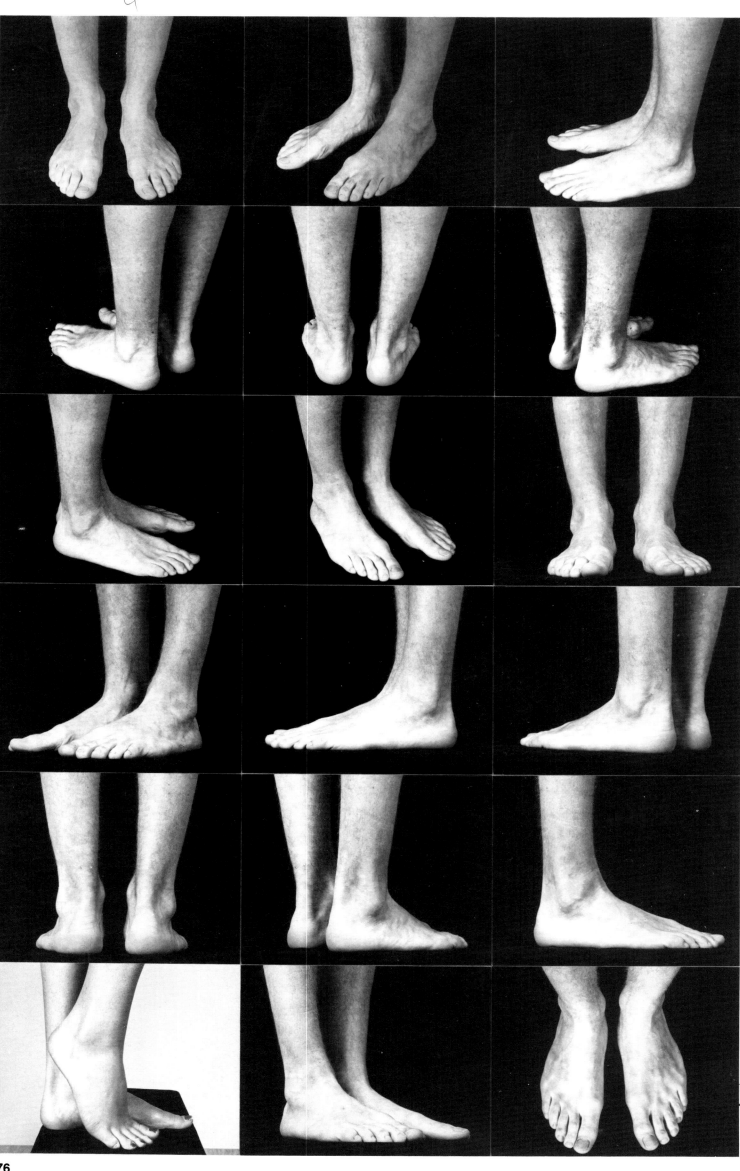

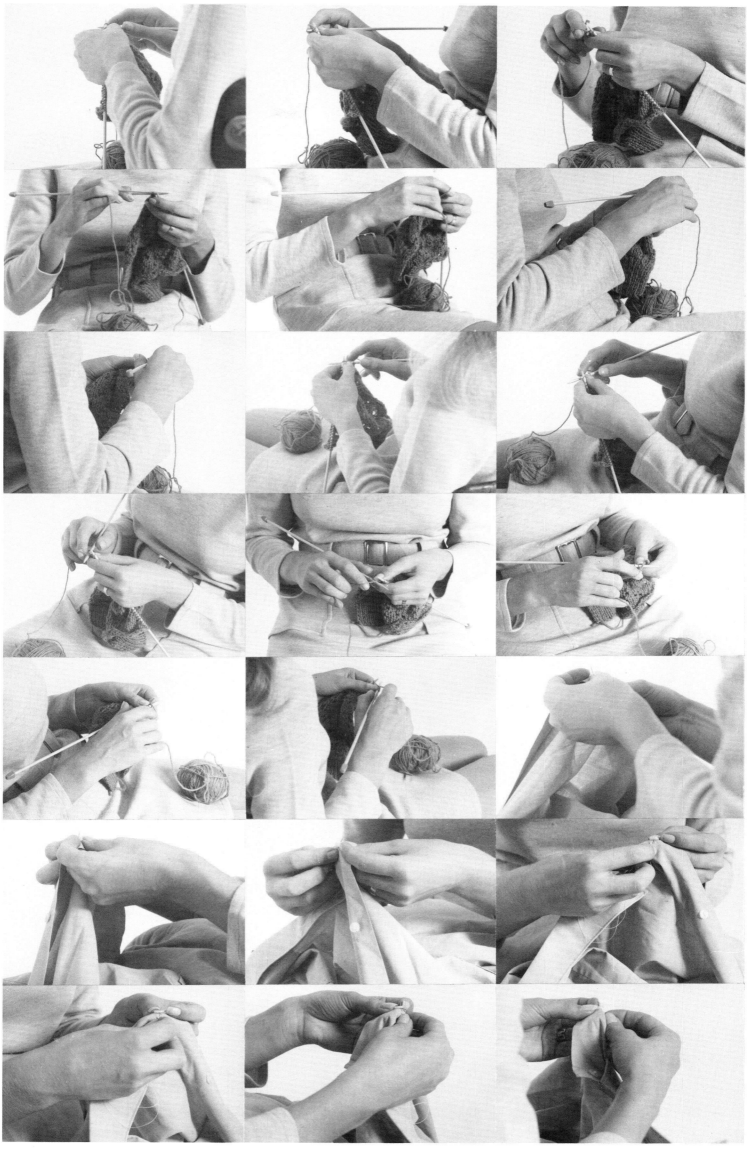

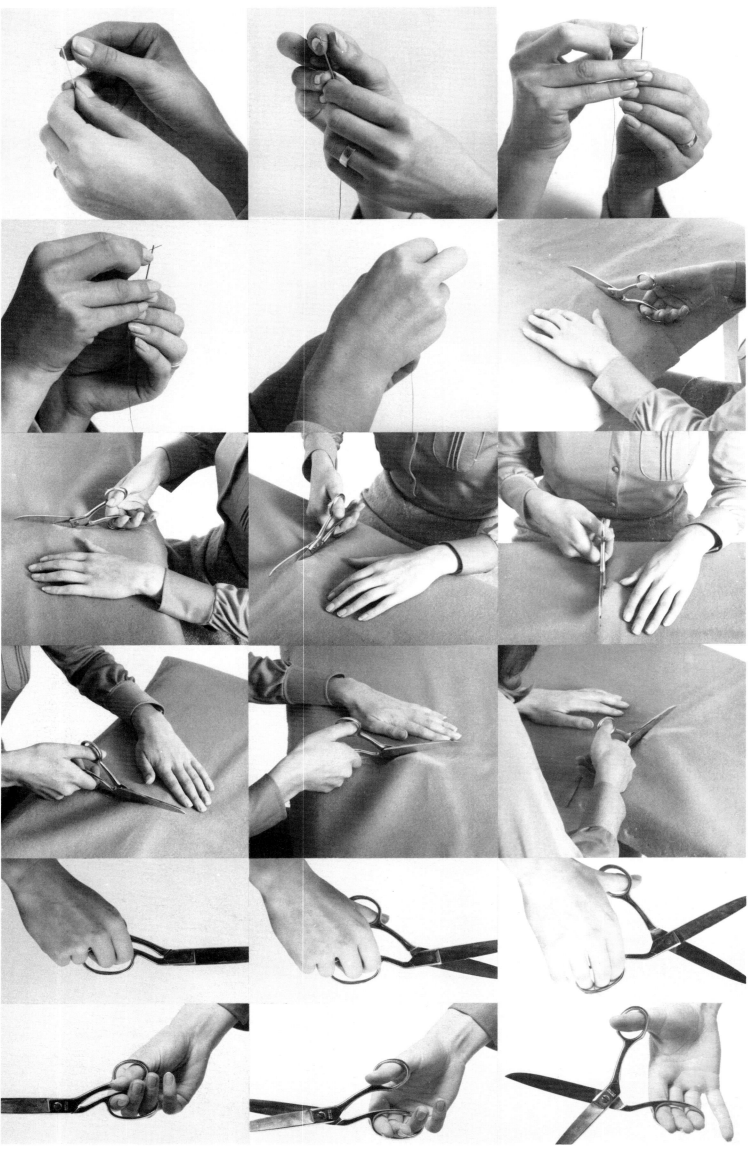

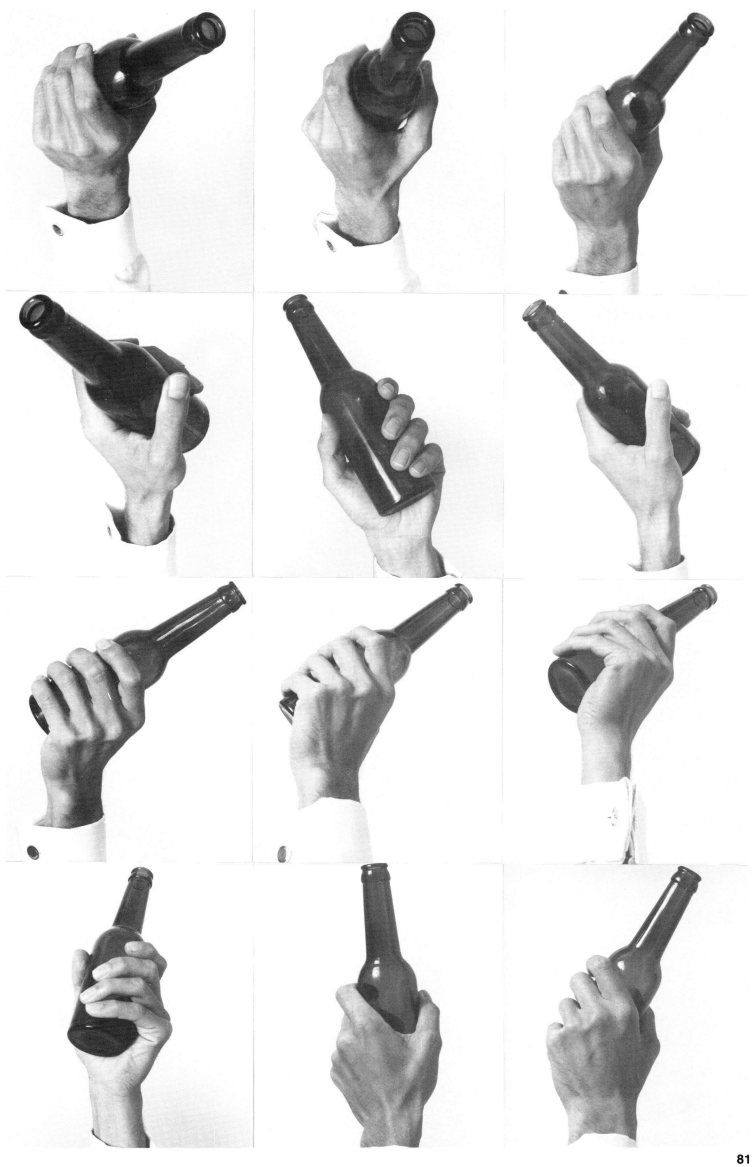

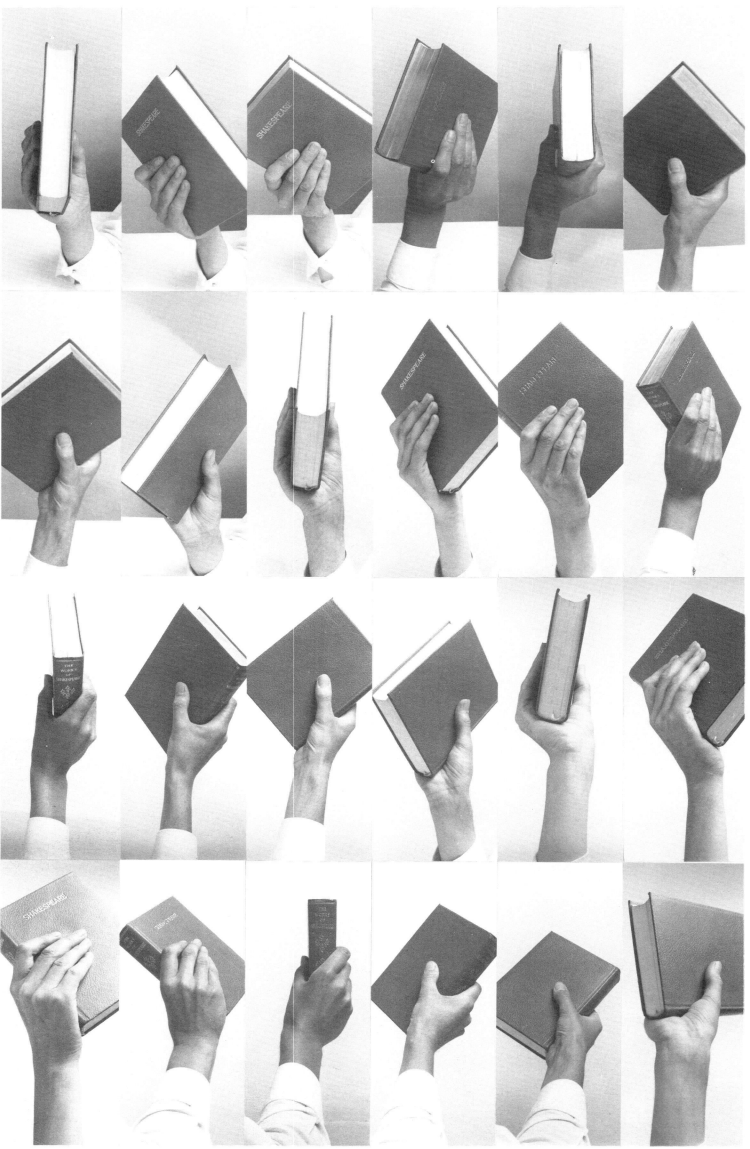

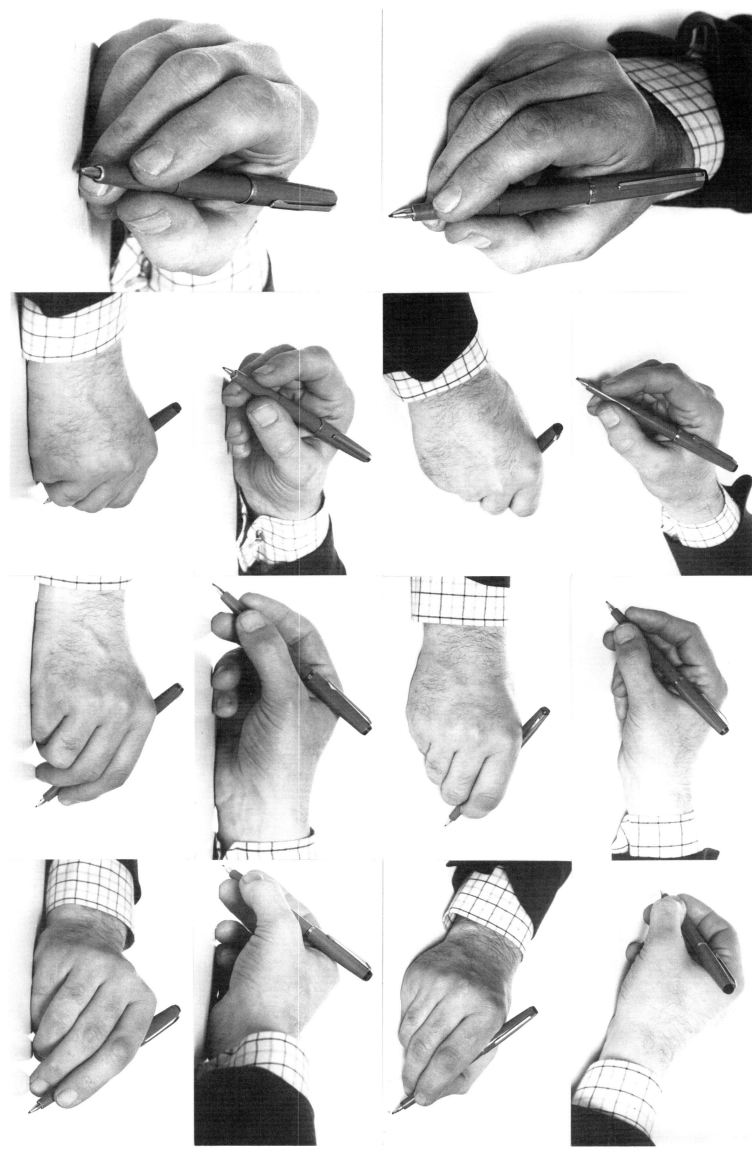

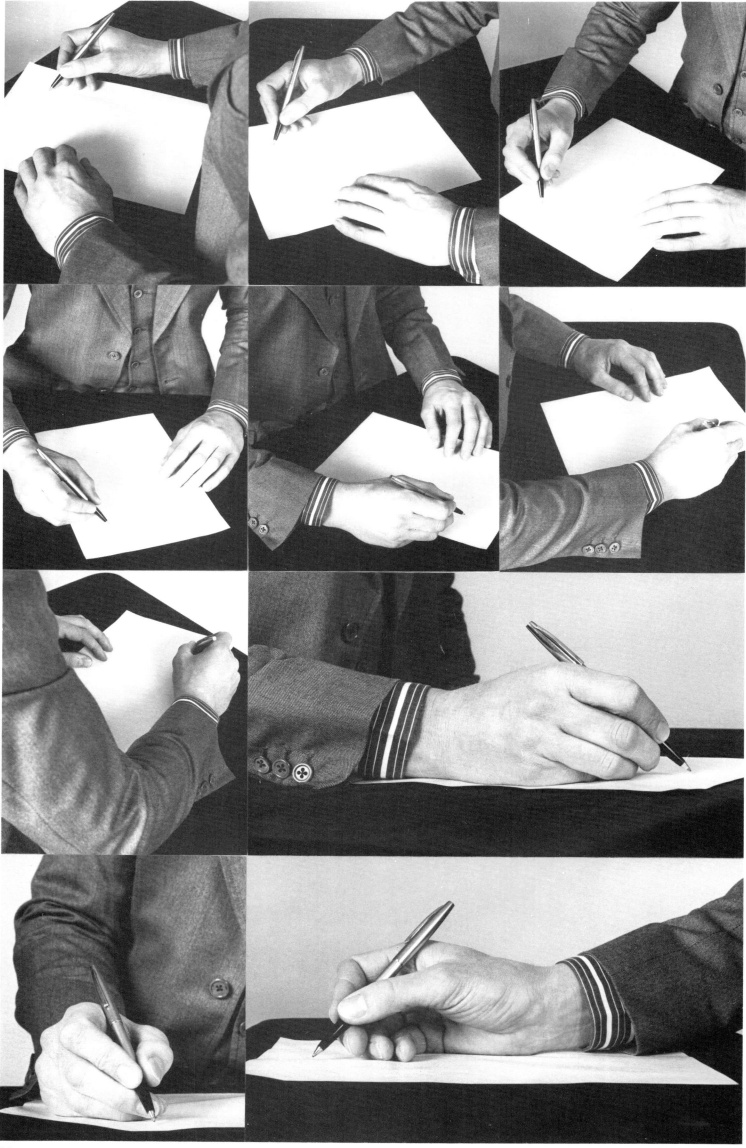

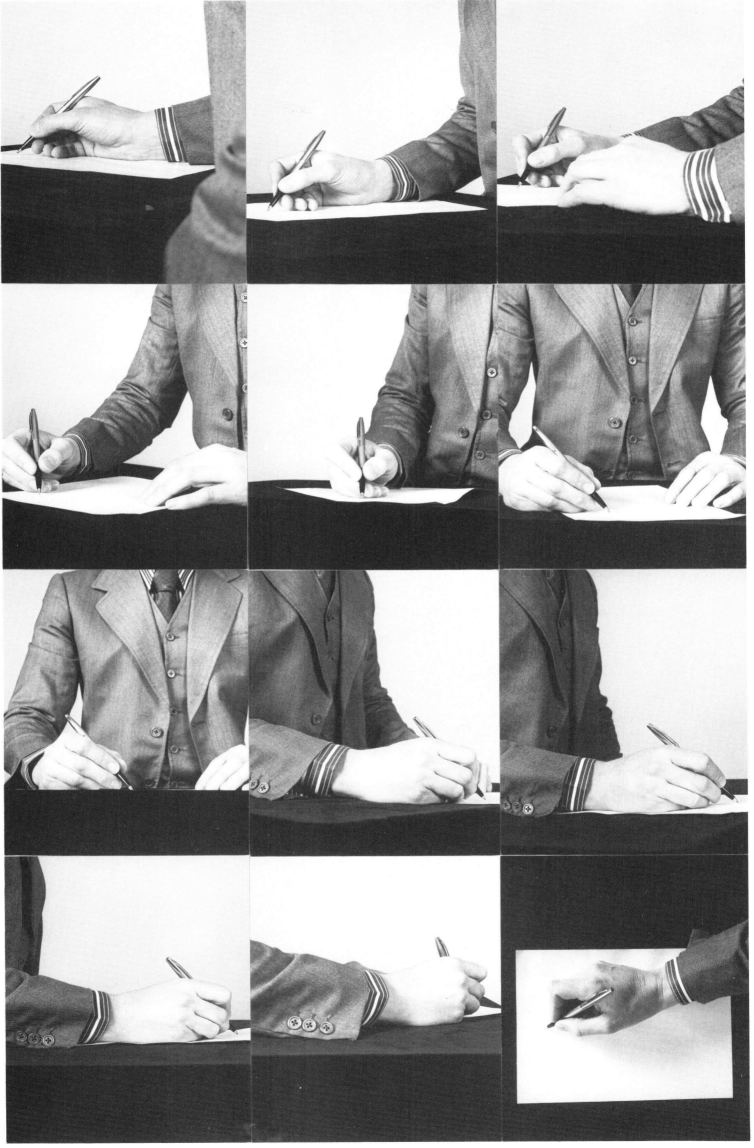

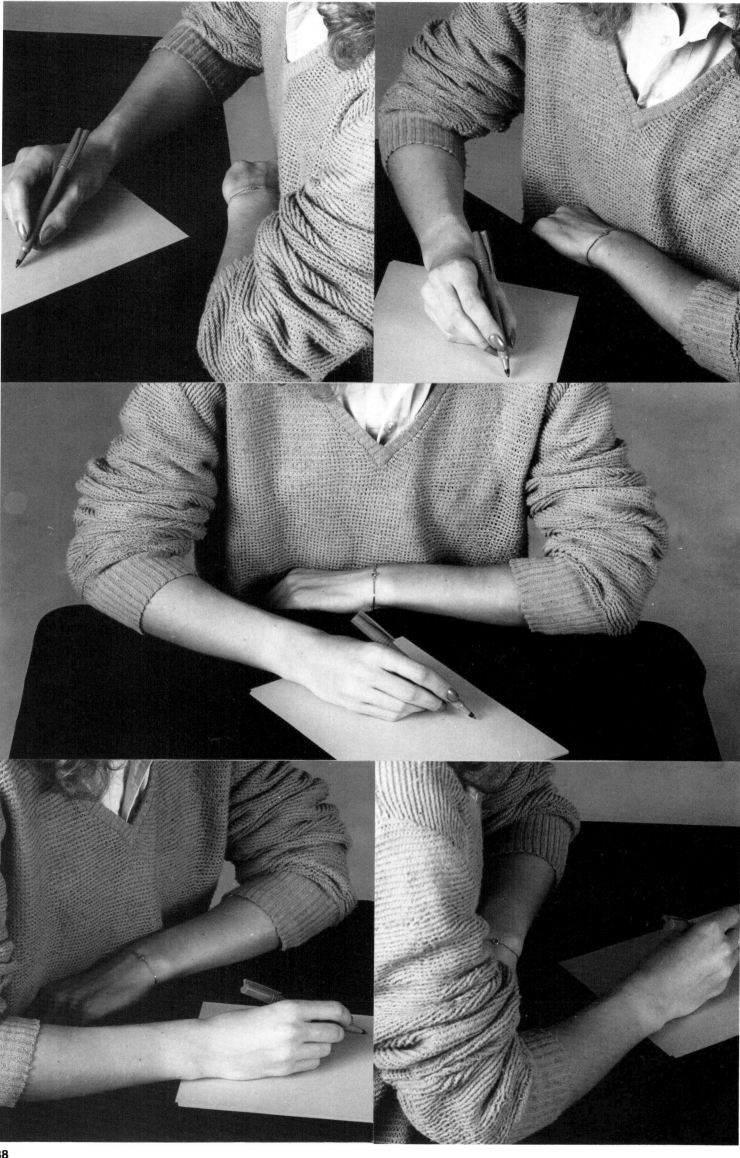

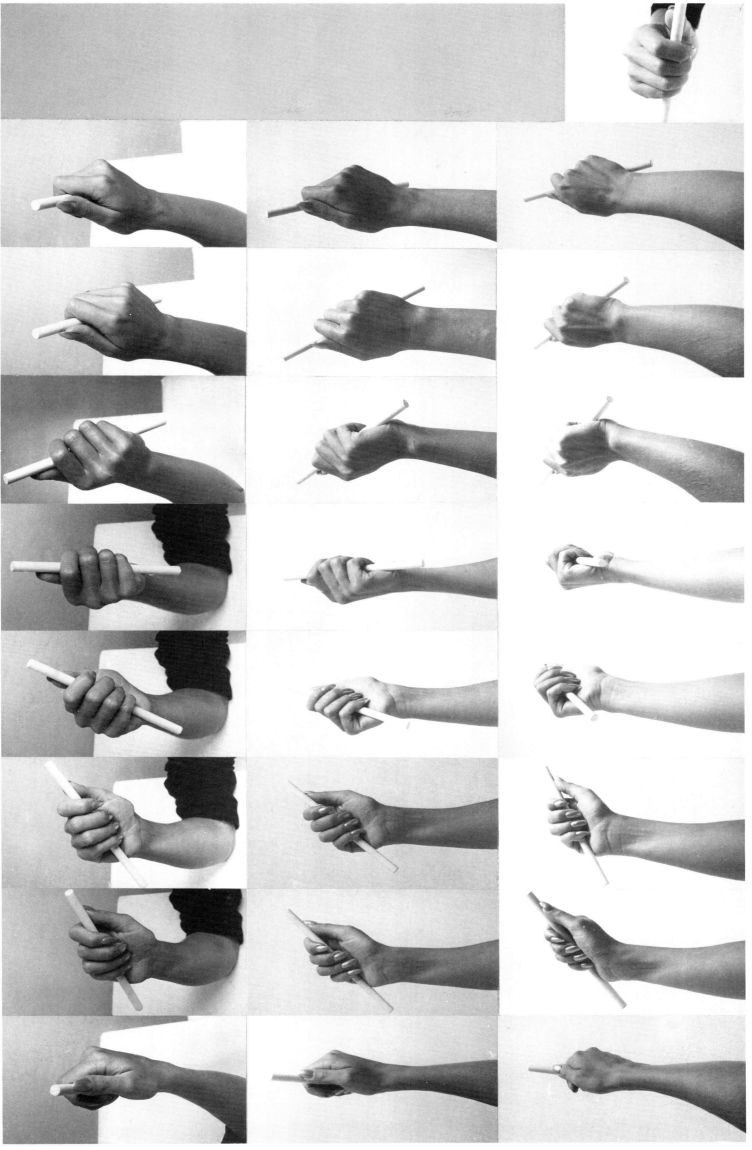

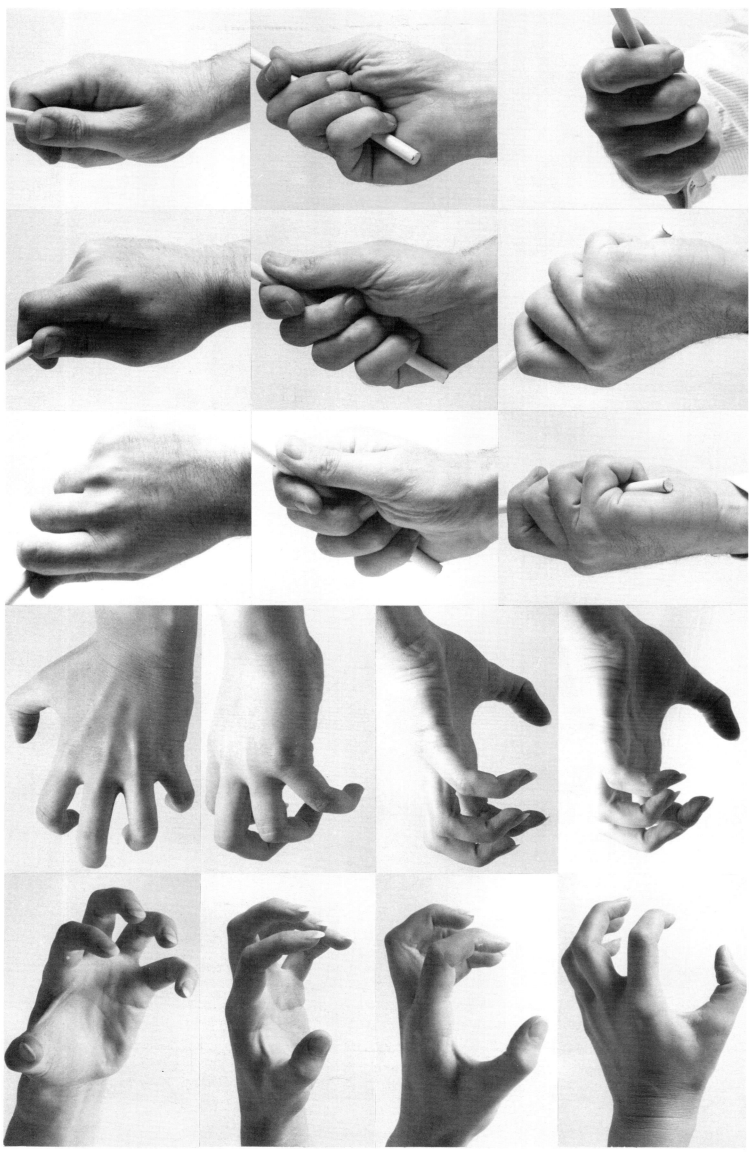

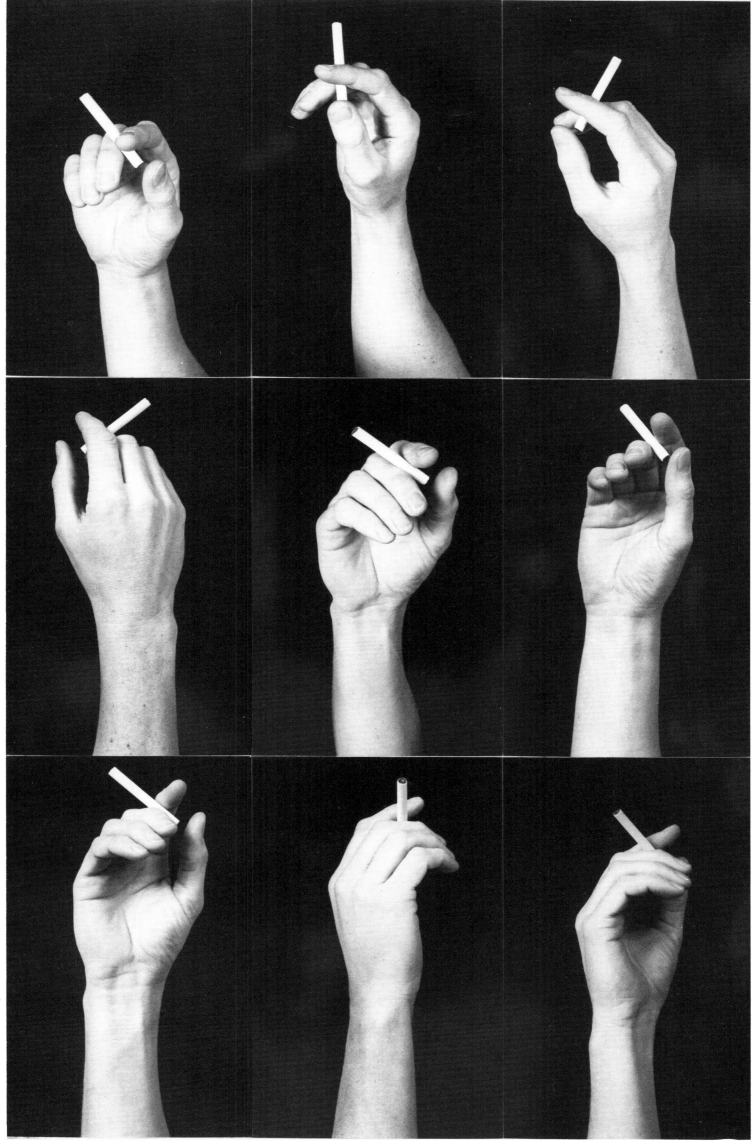

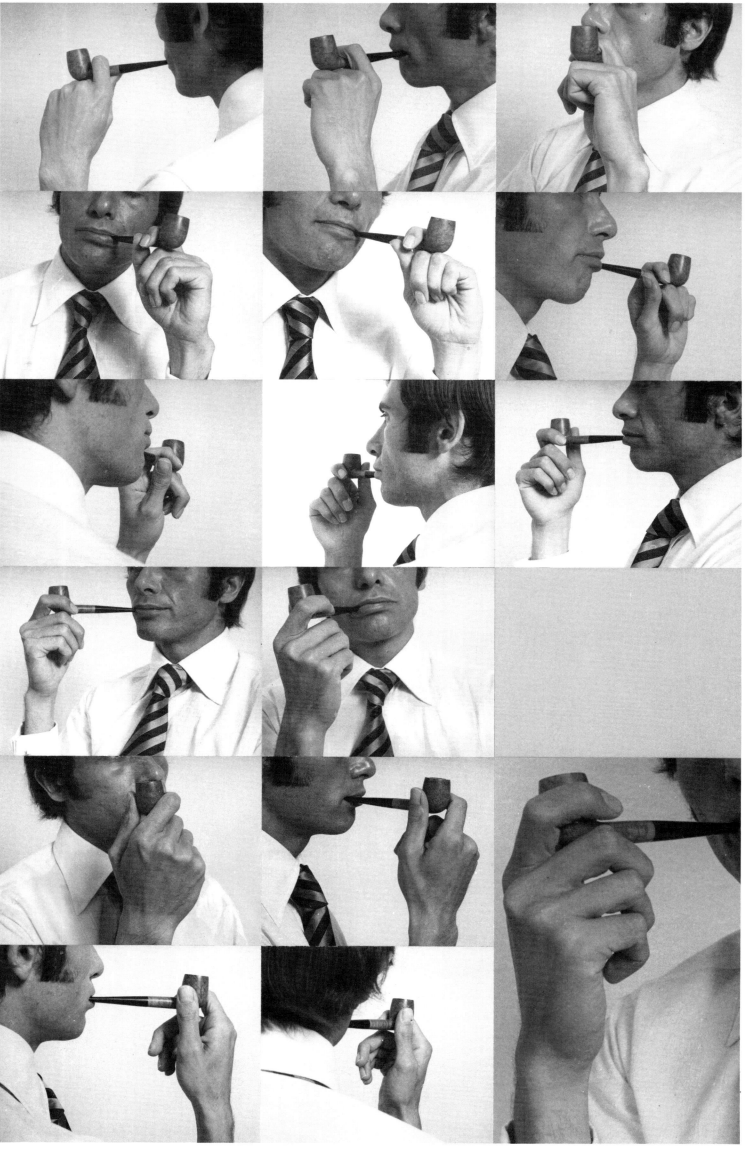

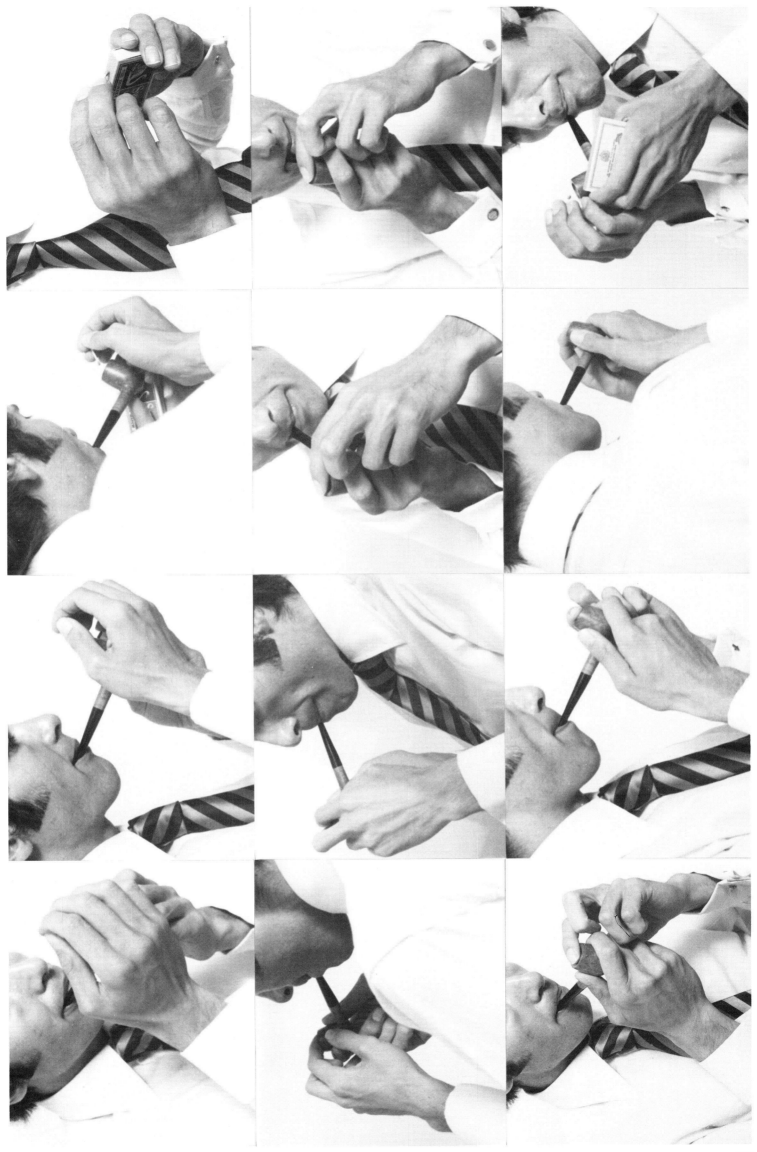

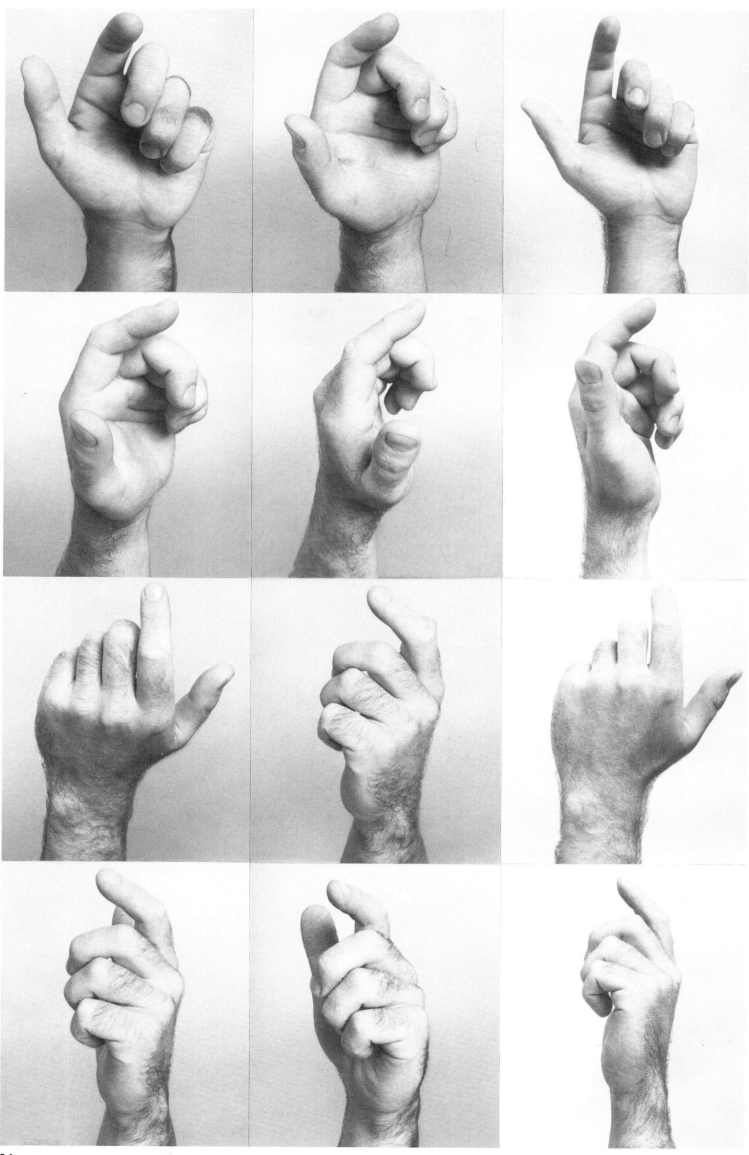

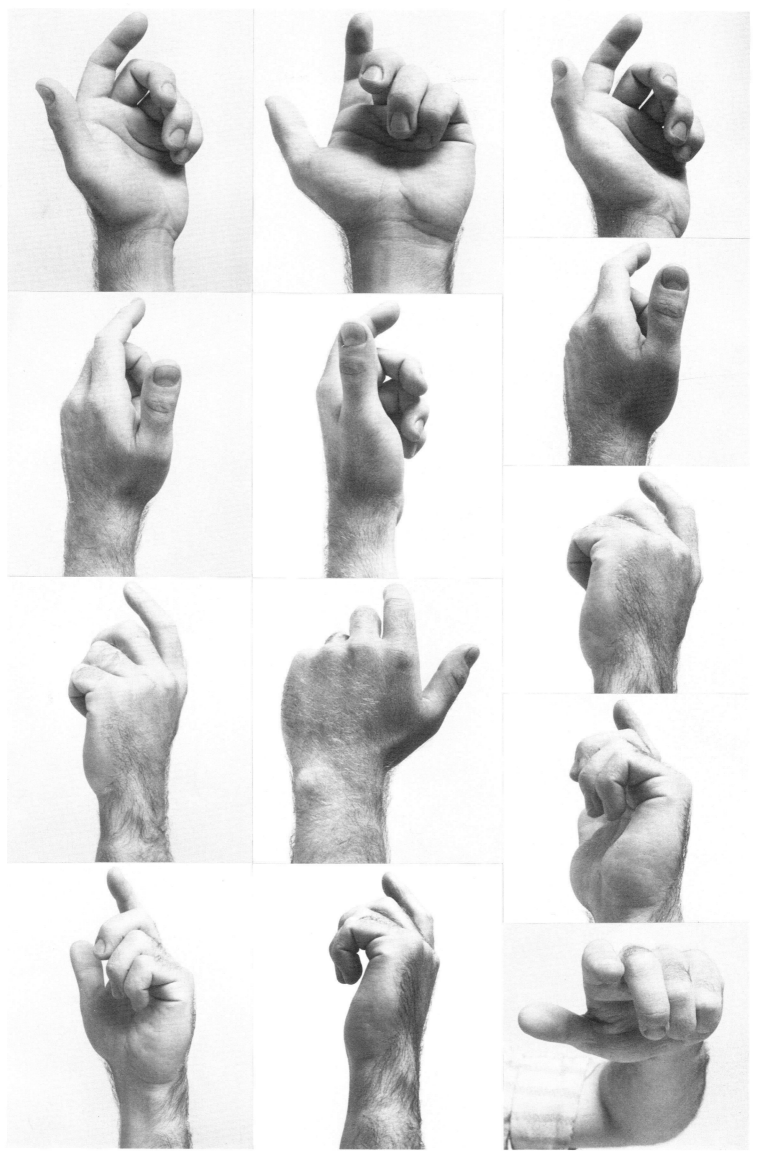

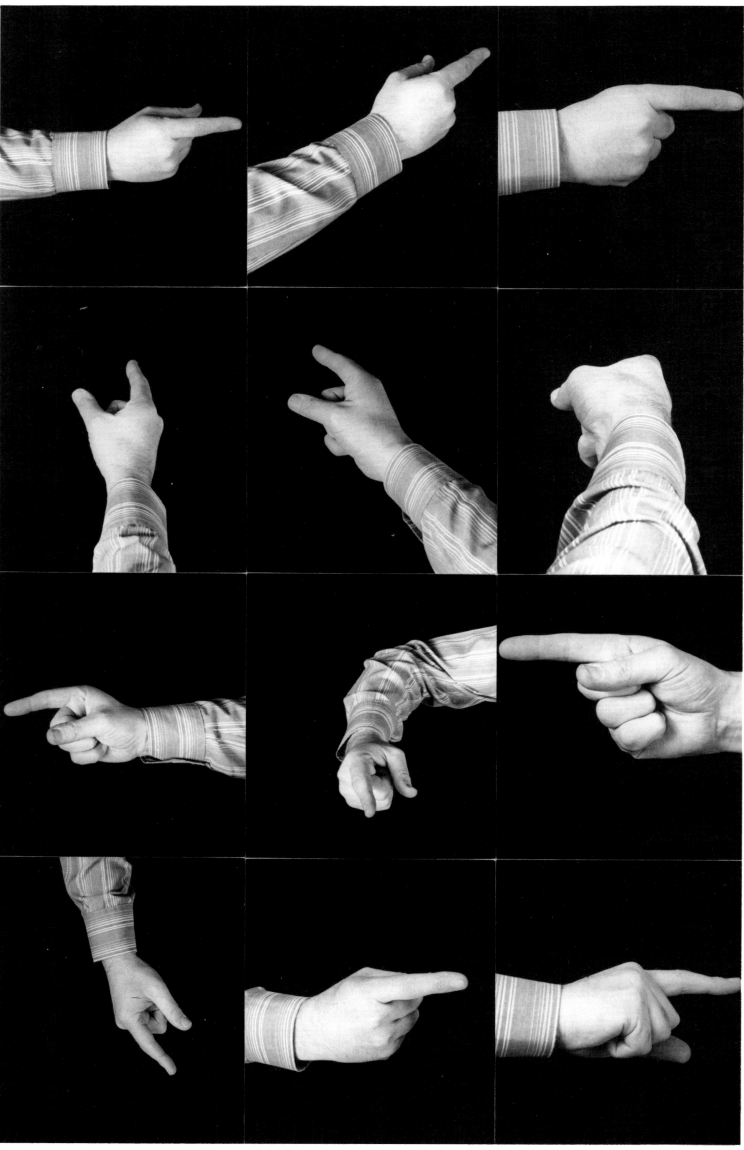

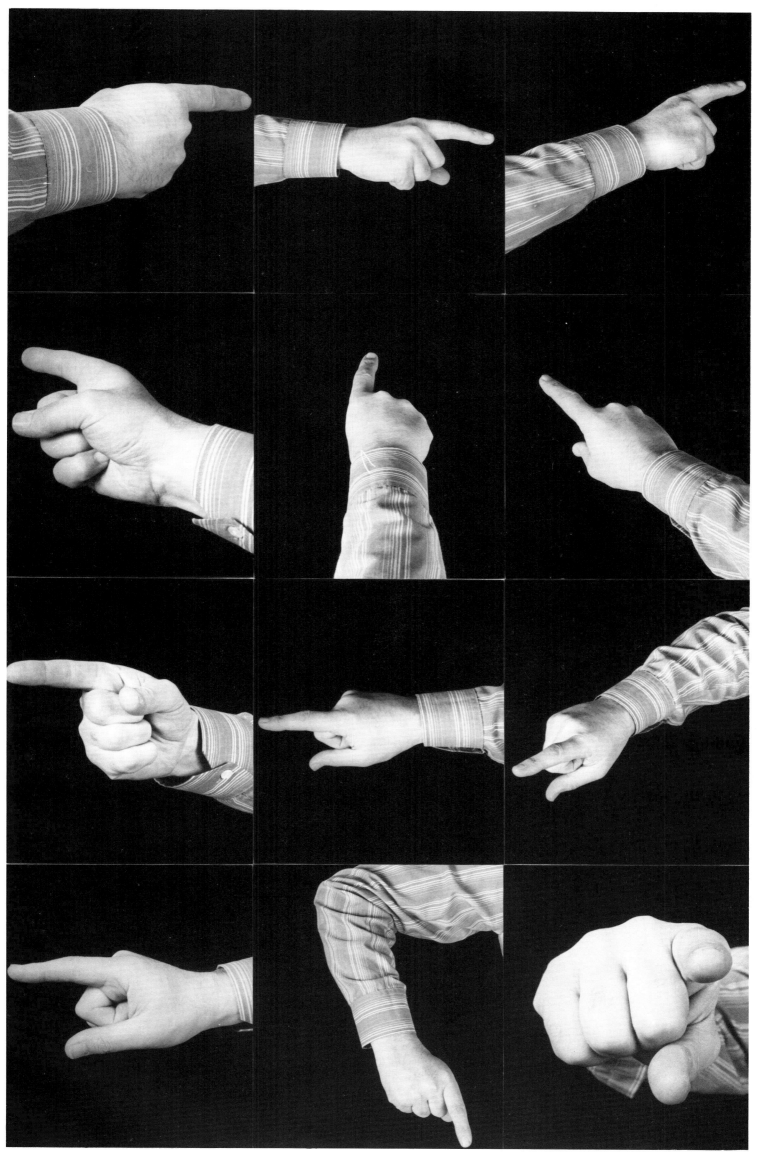

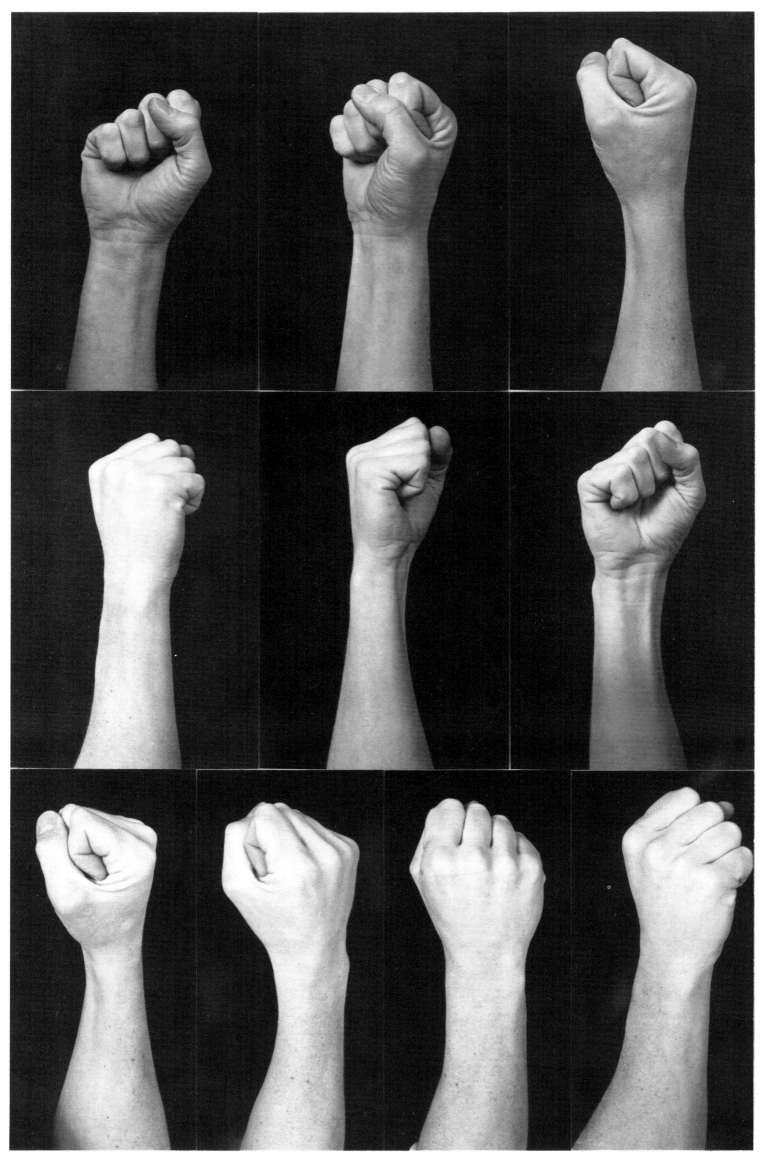

98

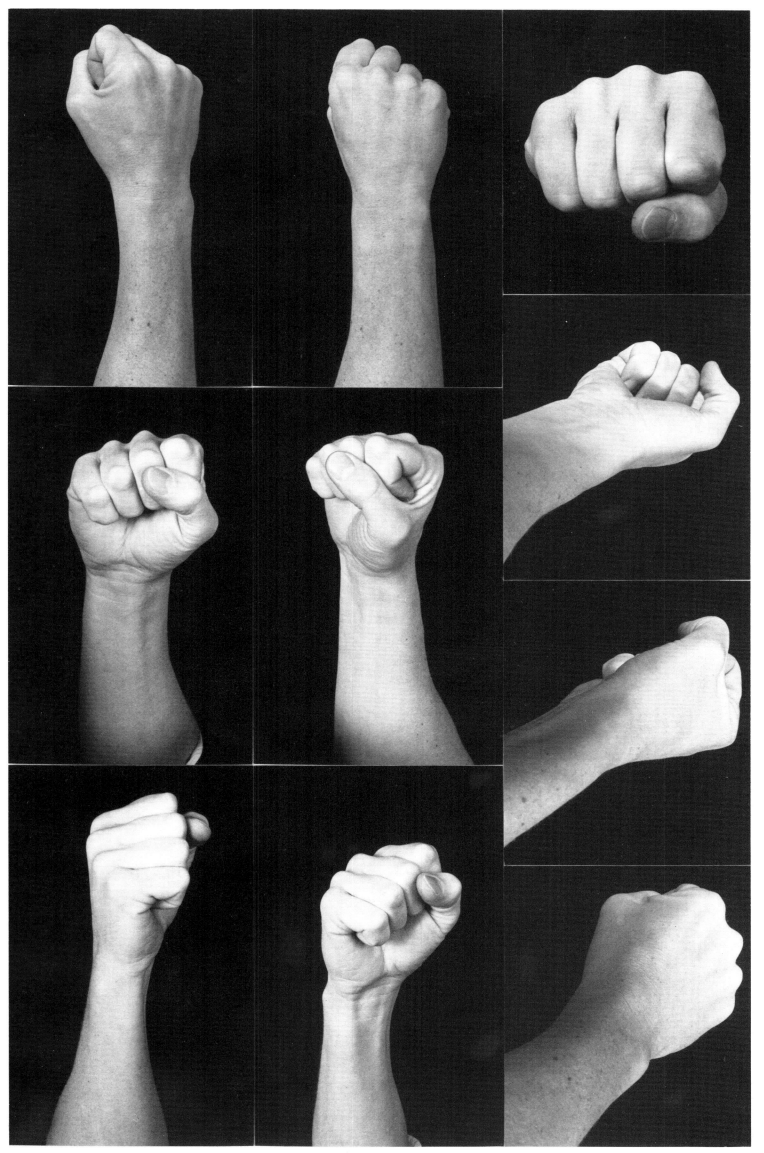

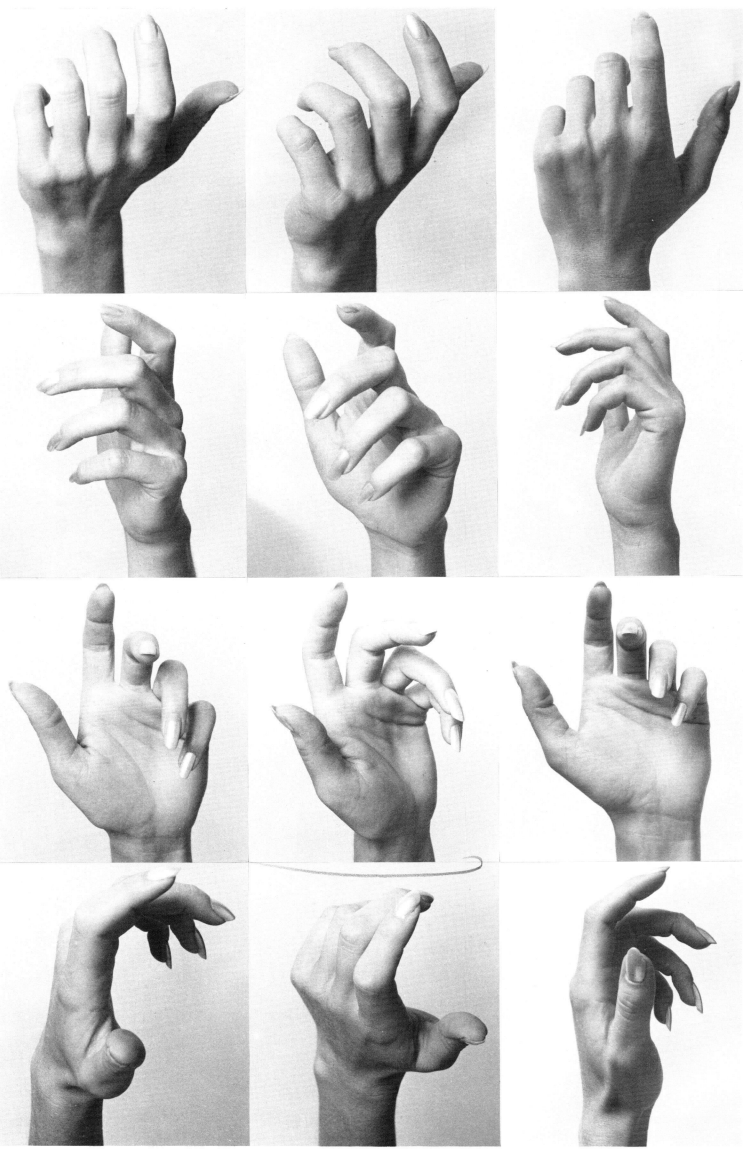

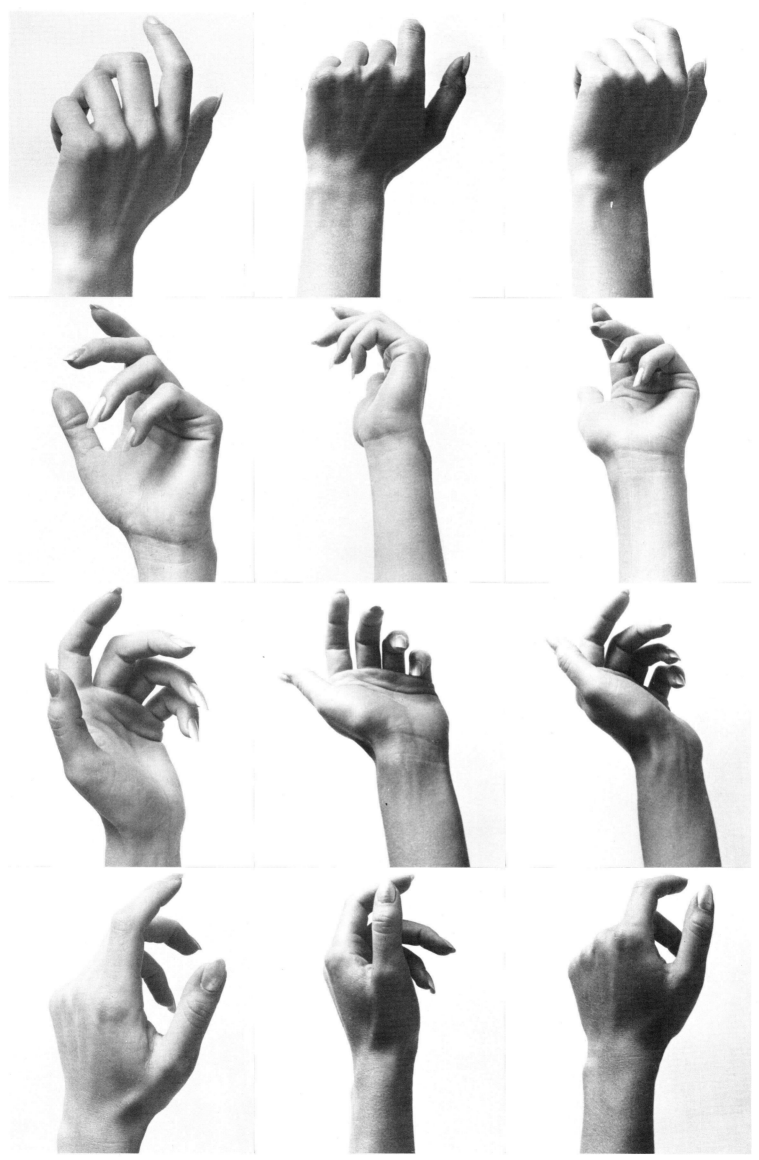

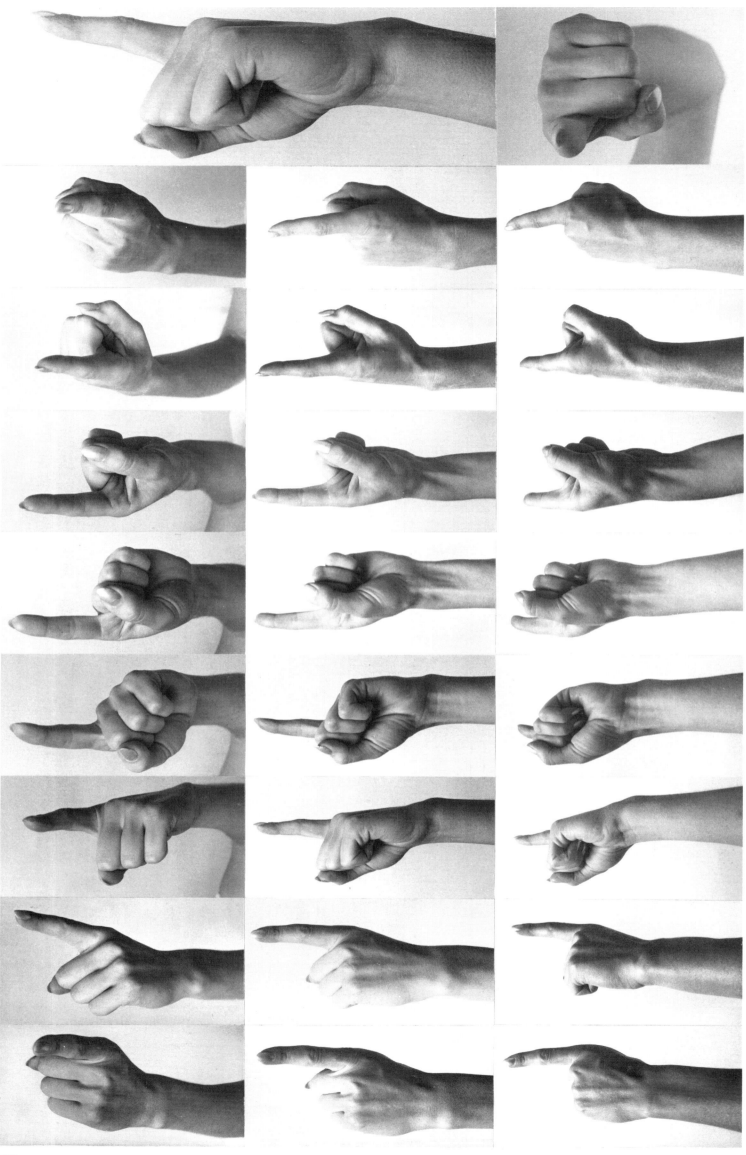

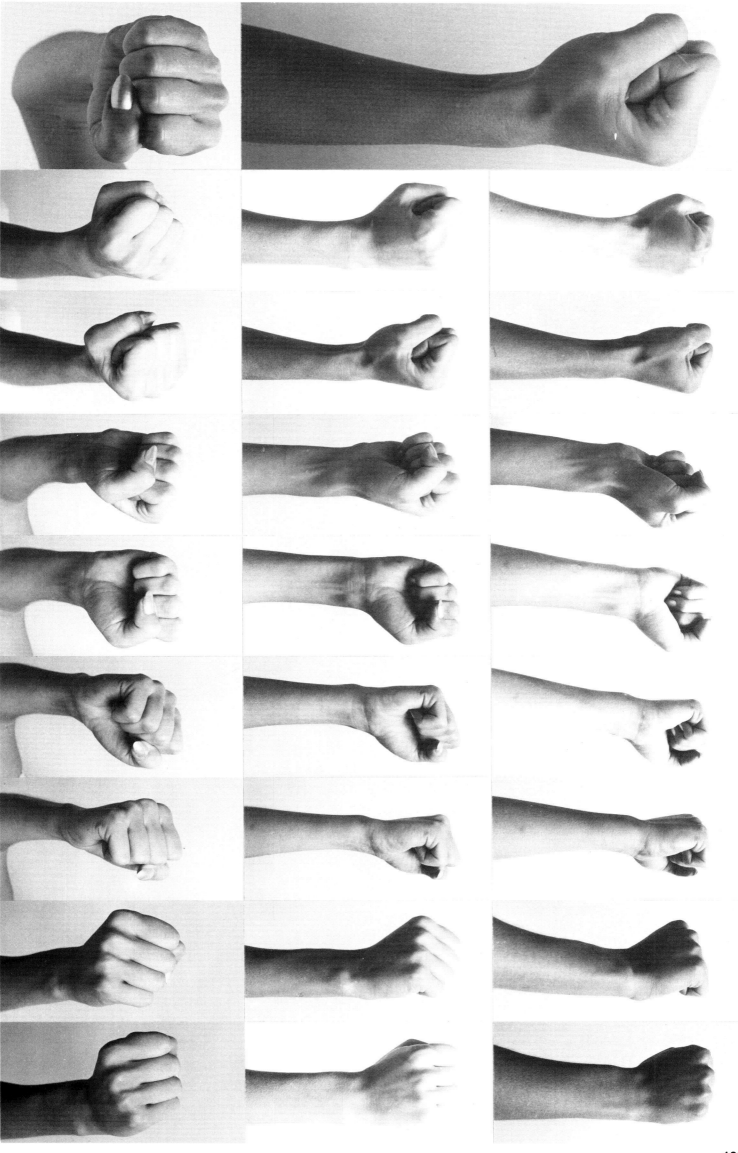

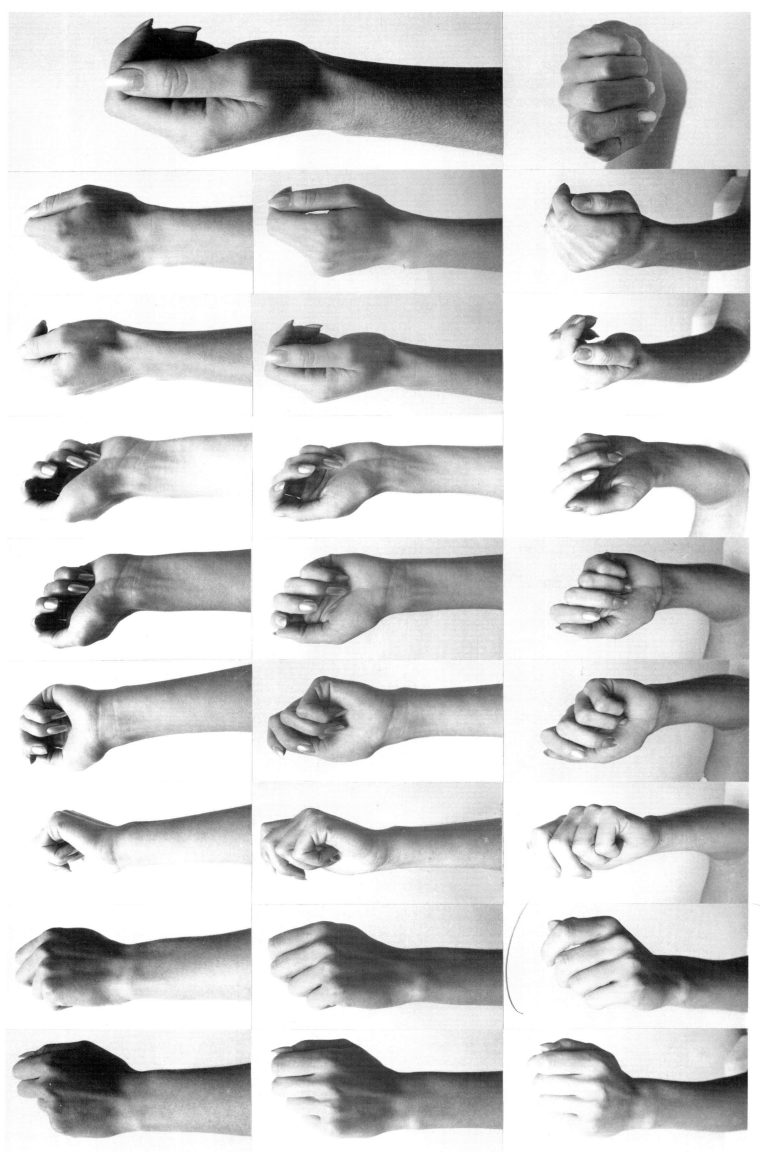

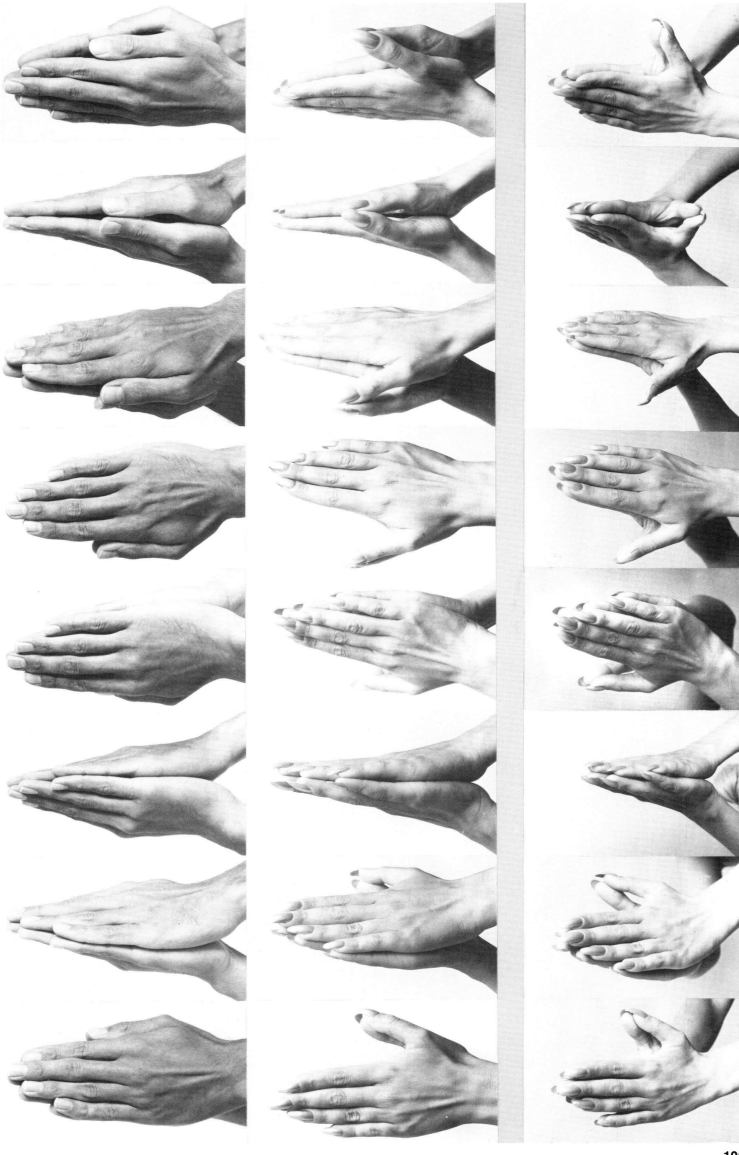

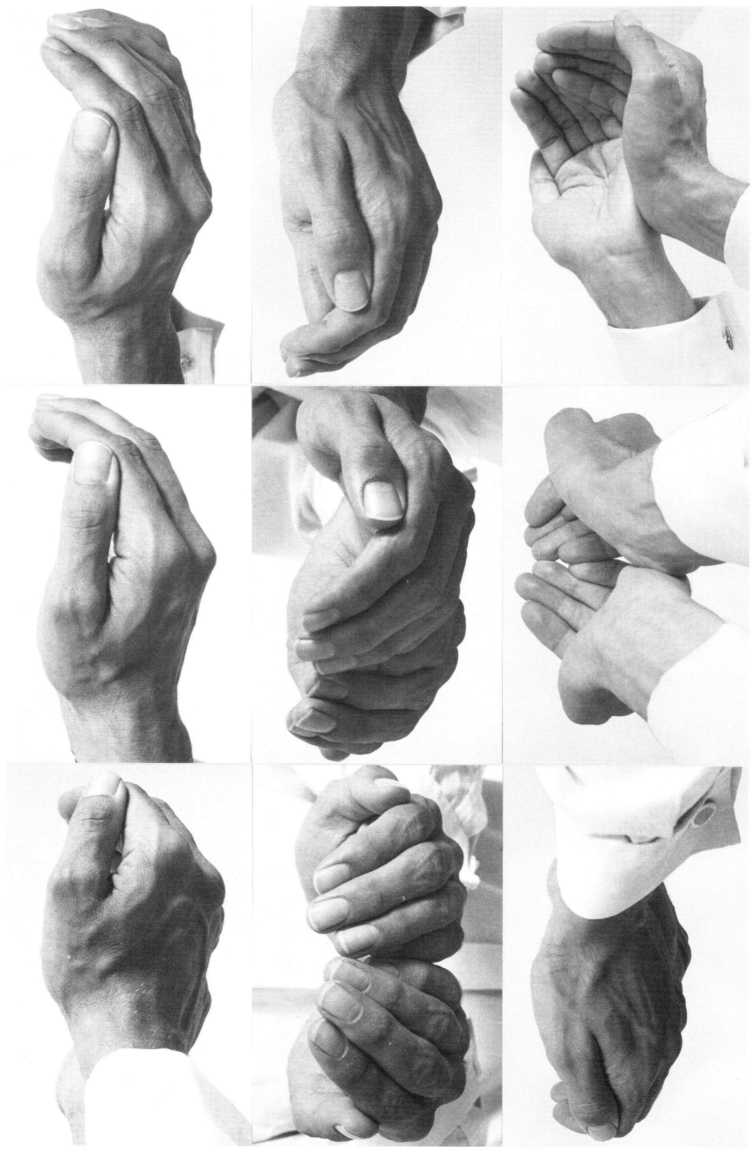

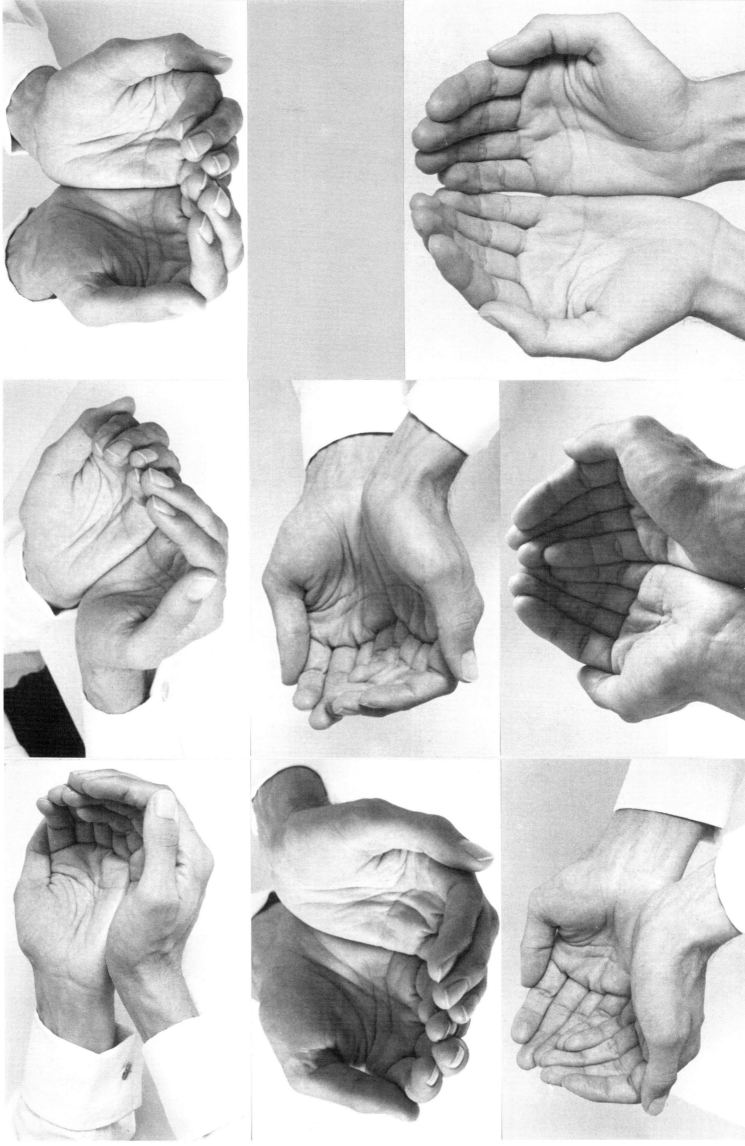

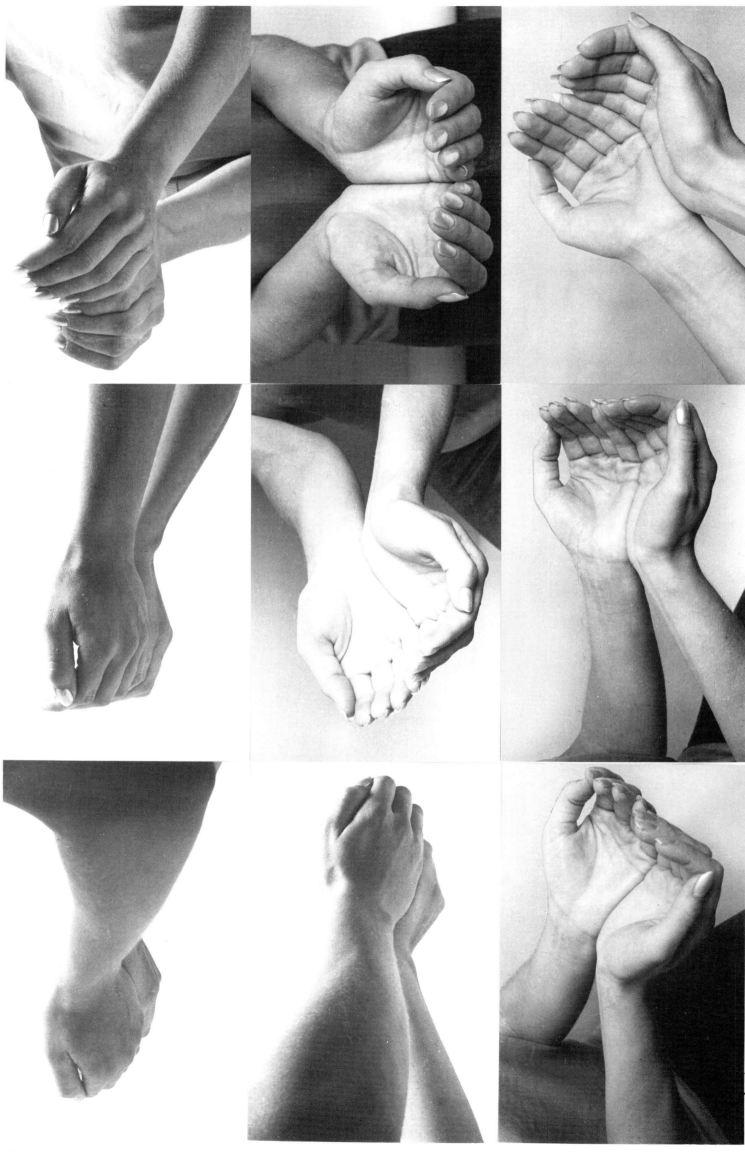

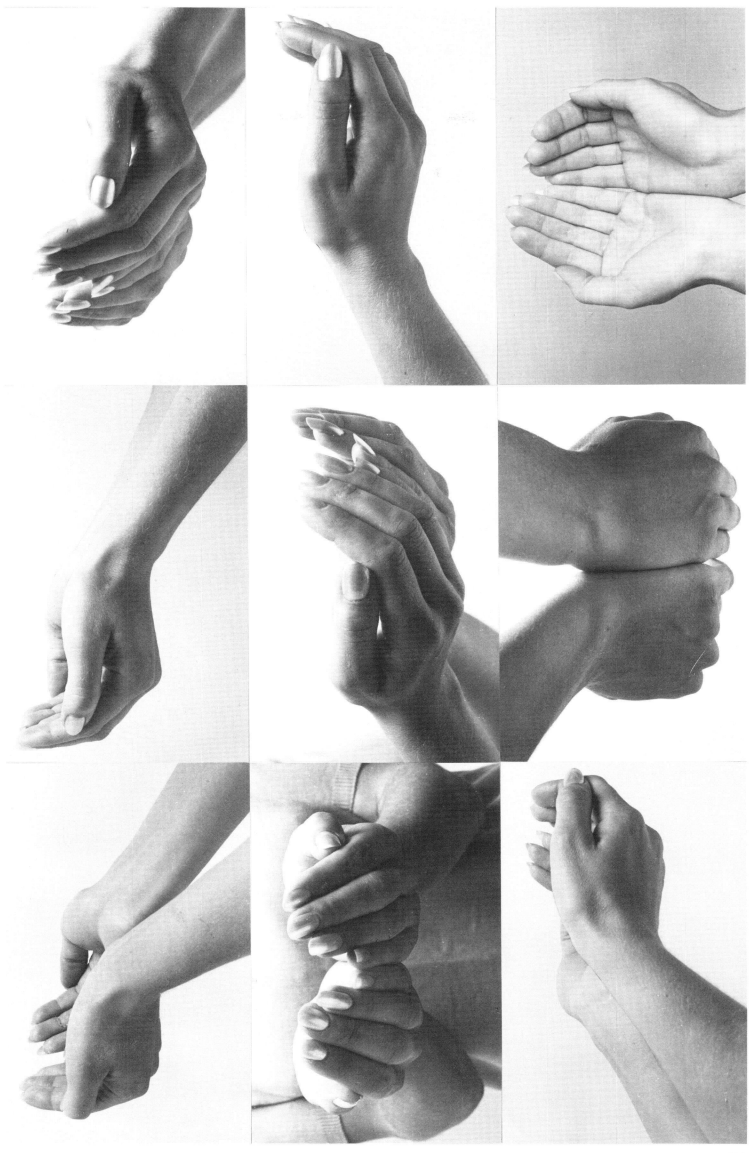

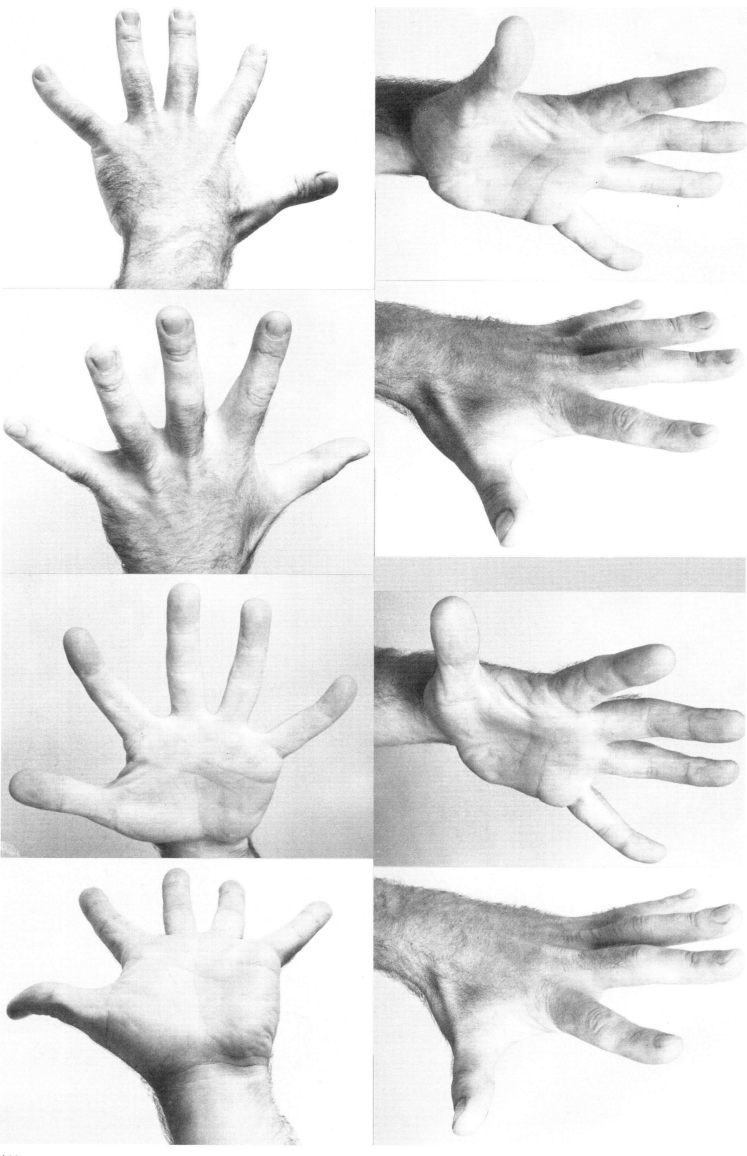

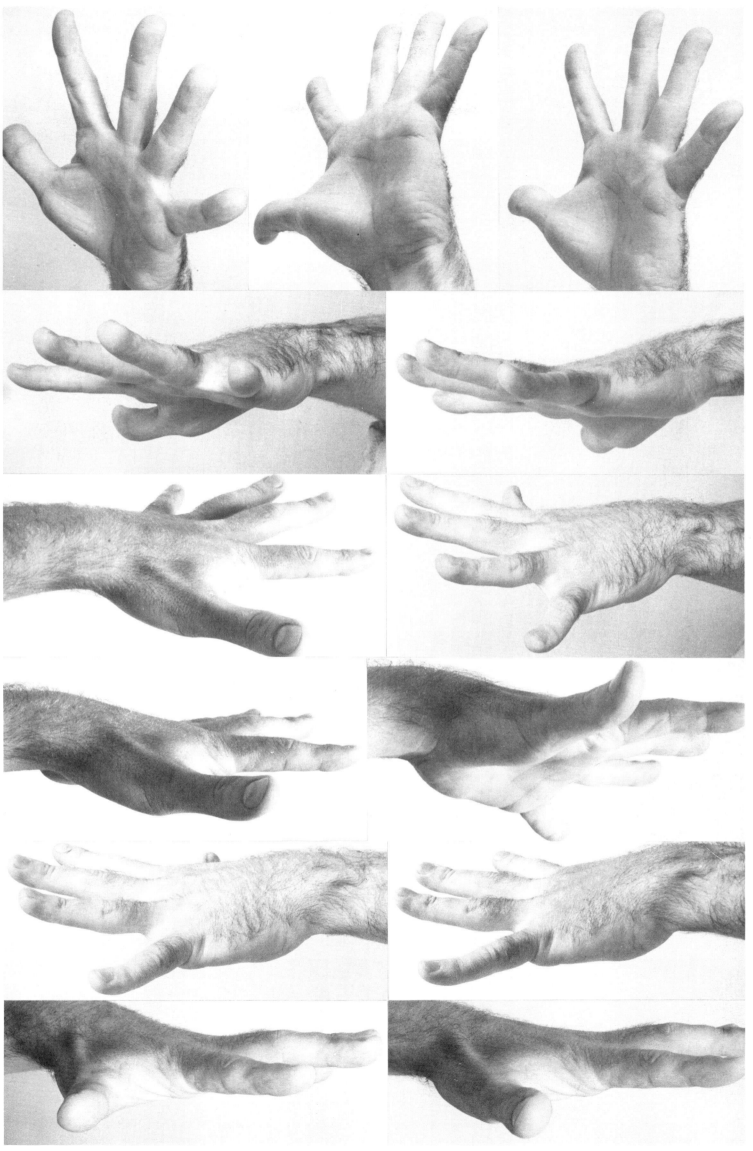

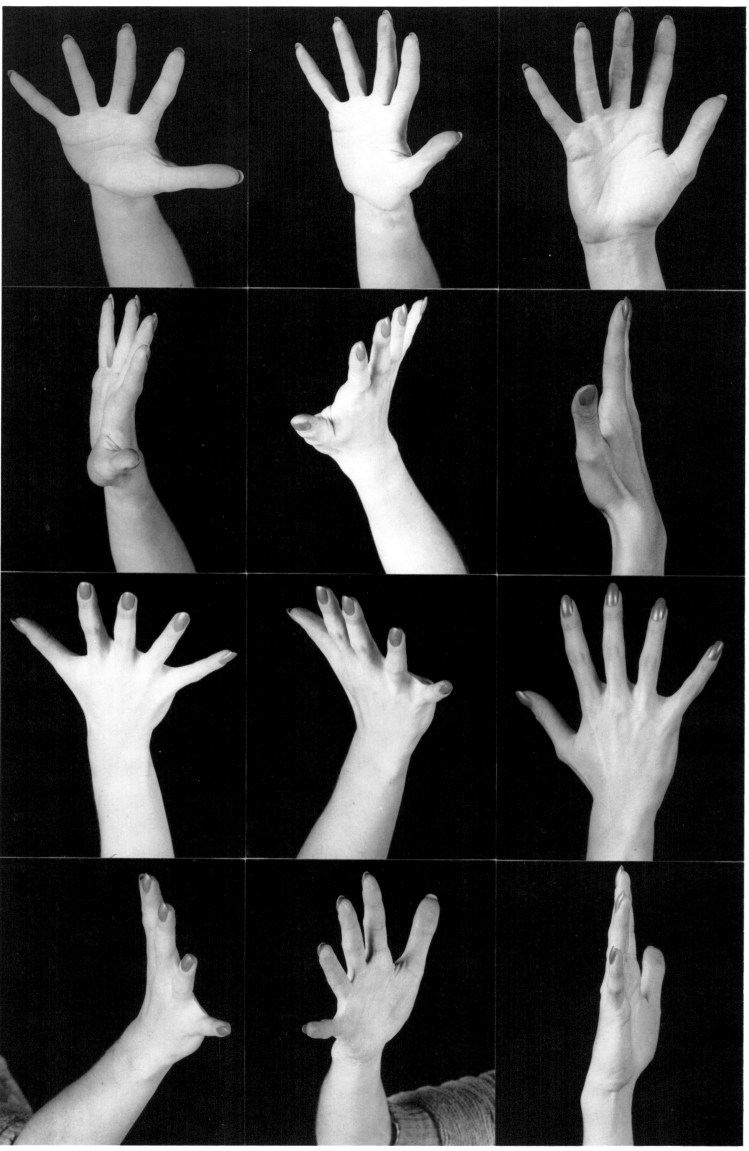

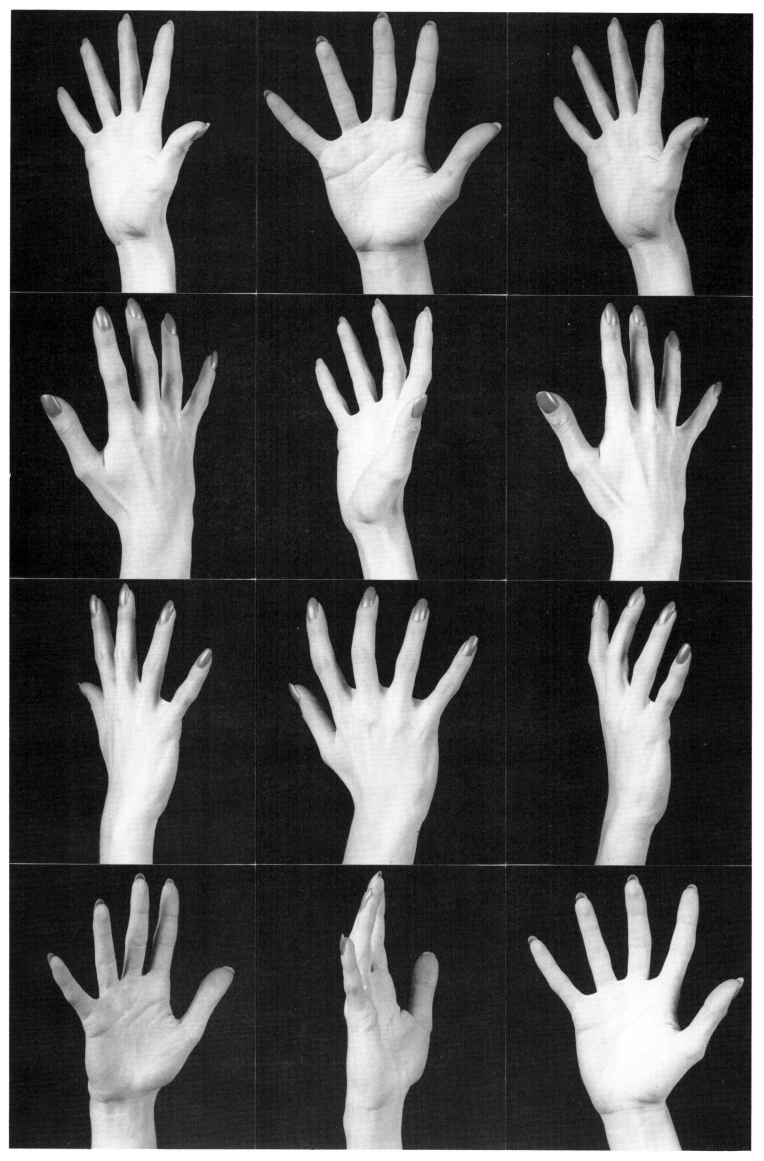

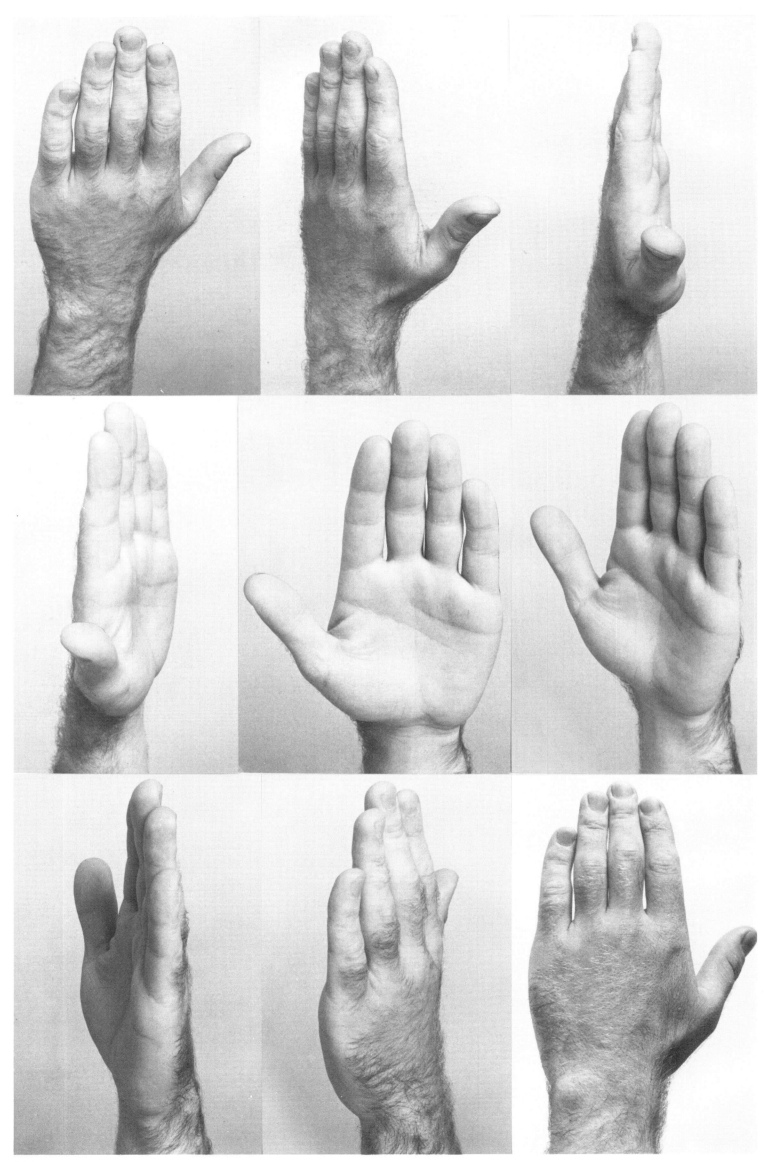

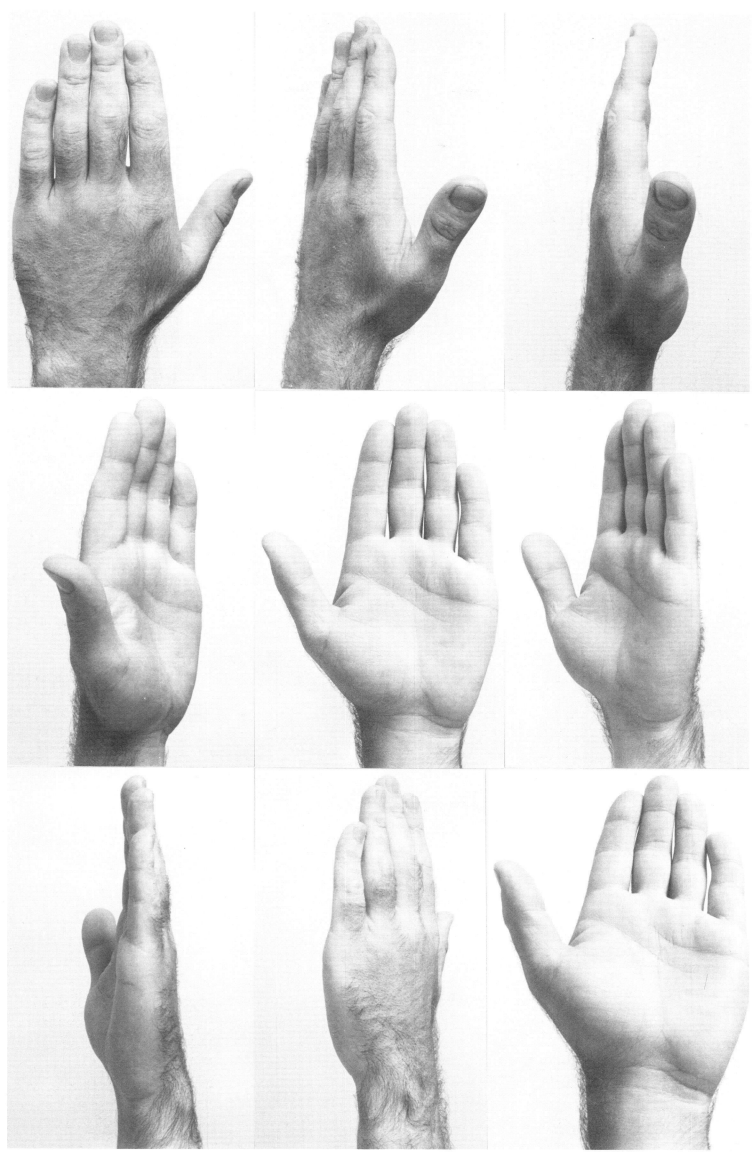

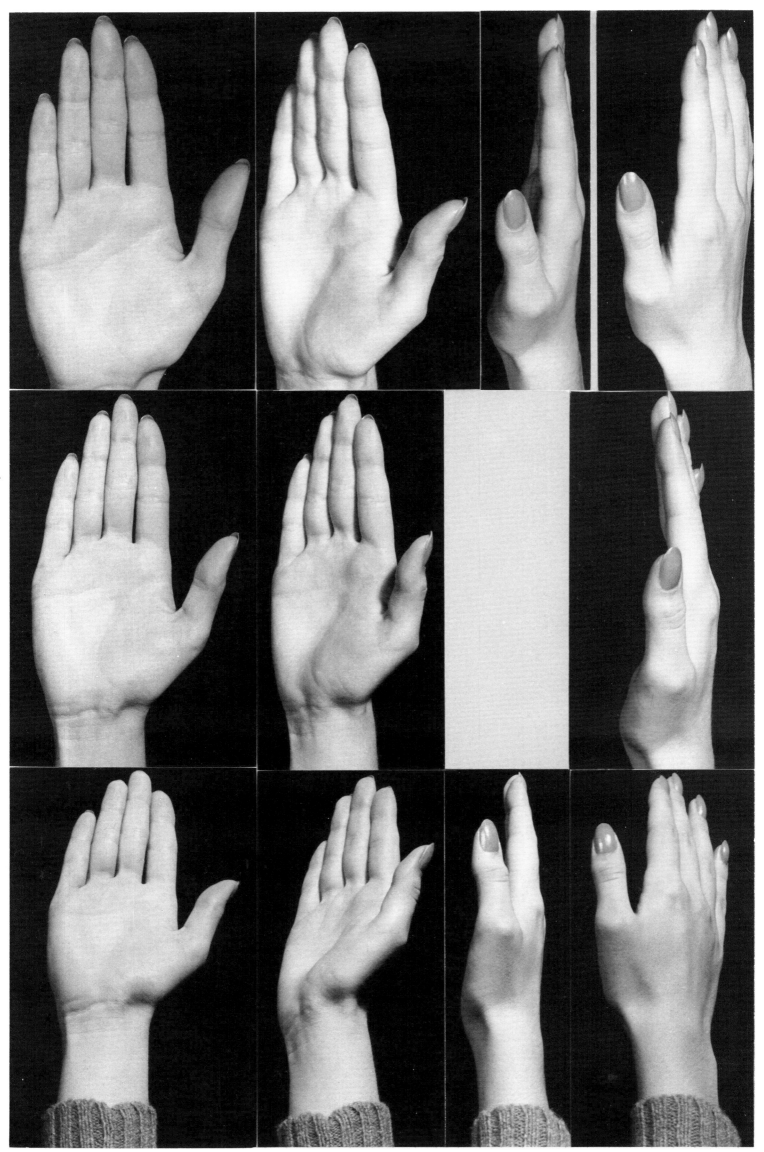

116

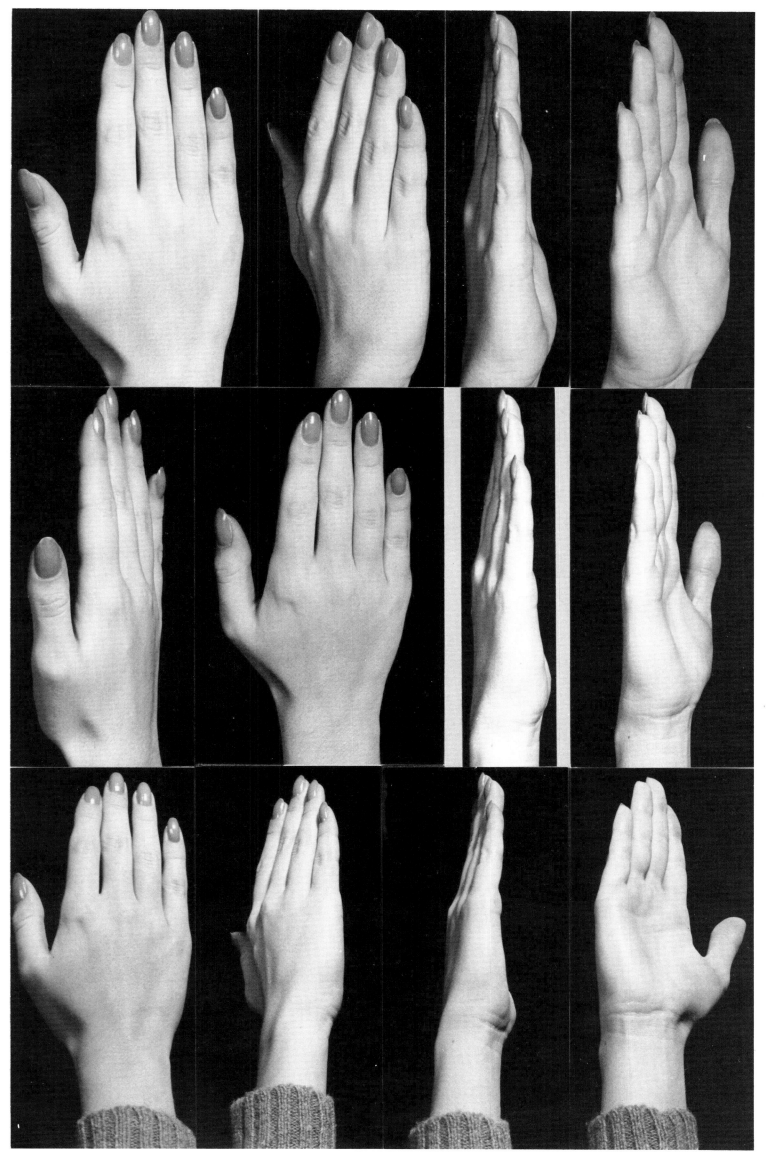

117

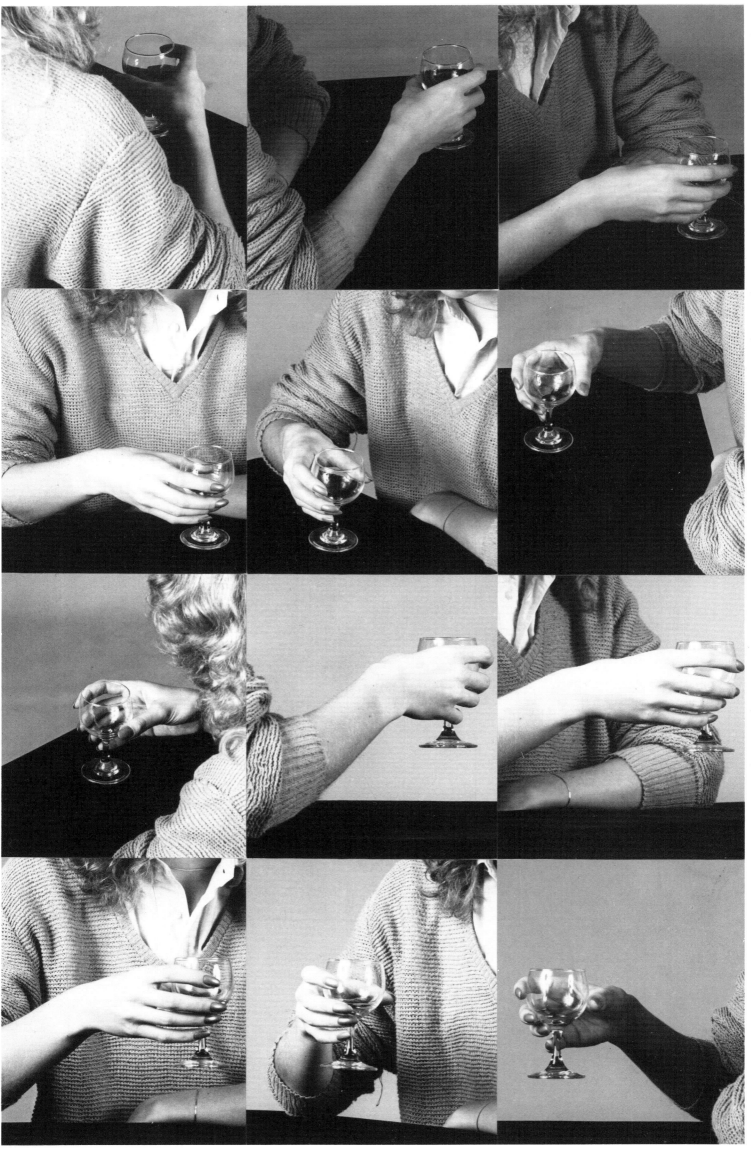

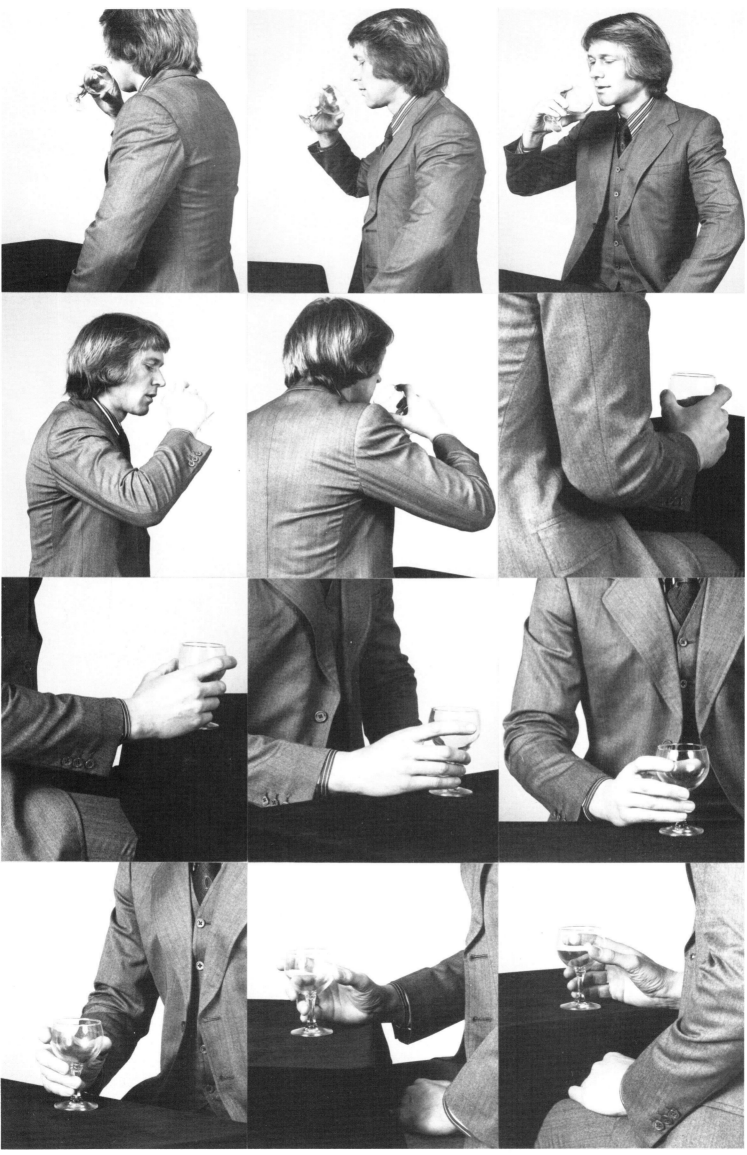

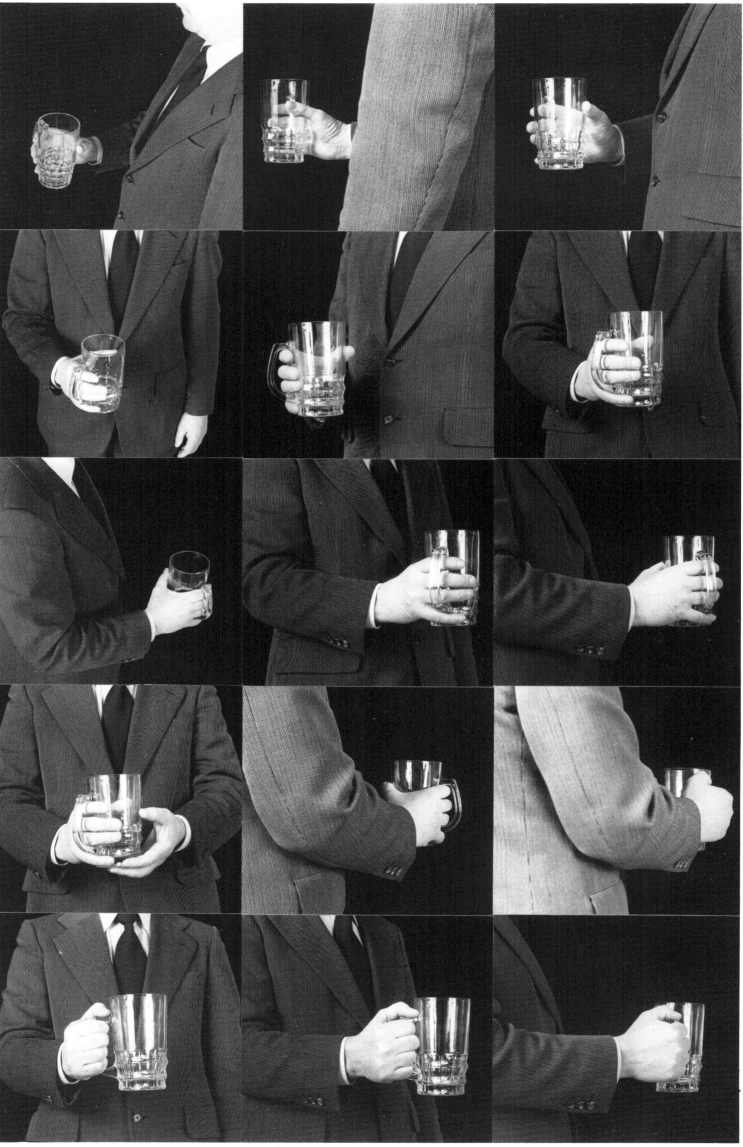

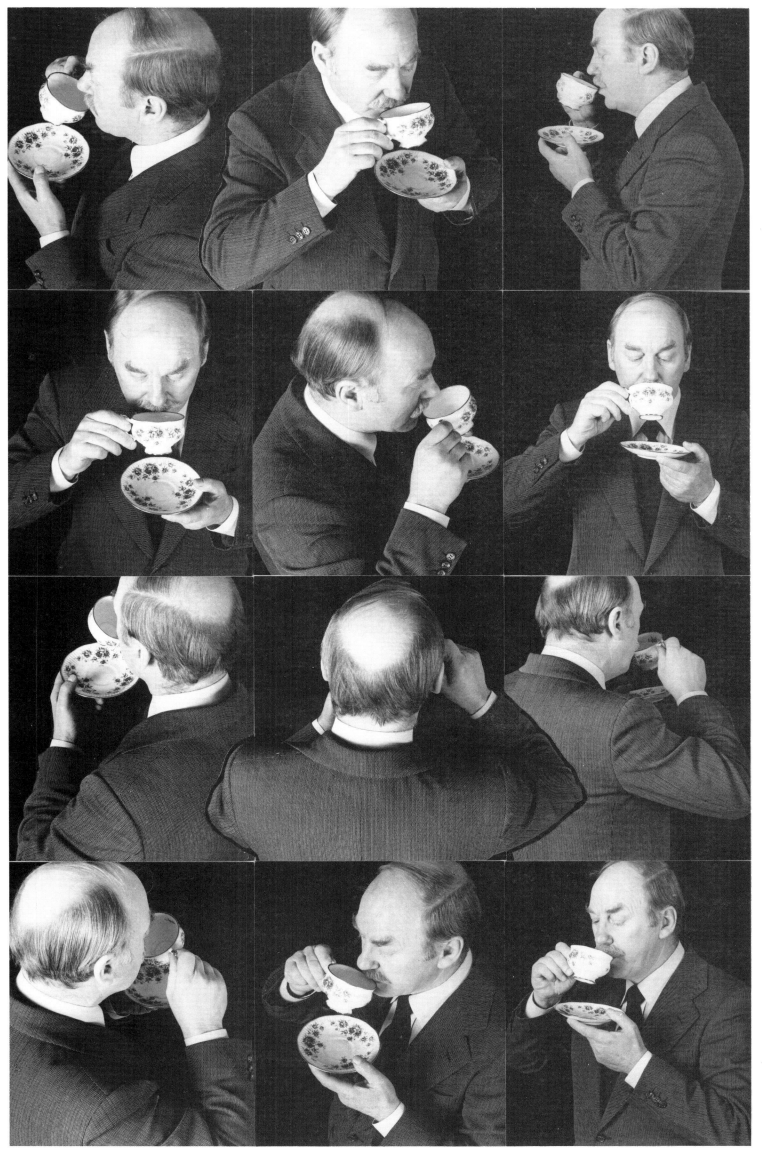

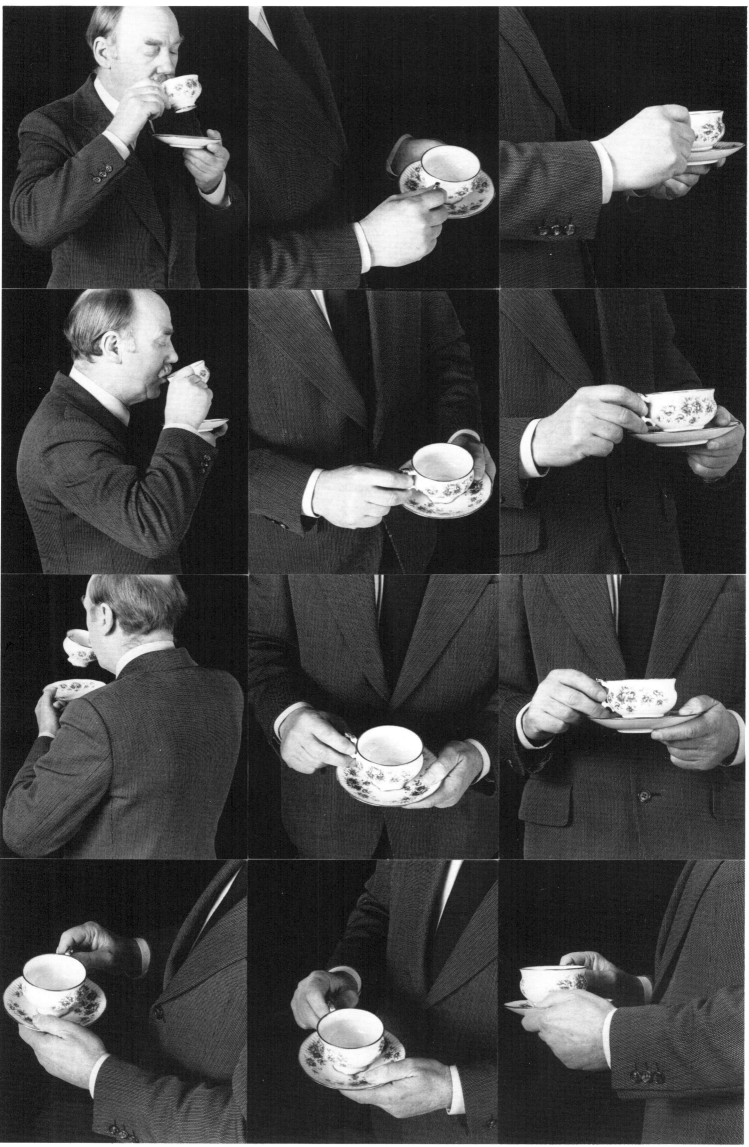

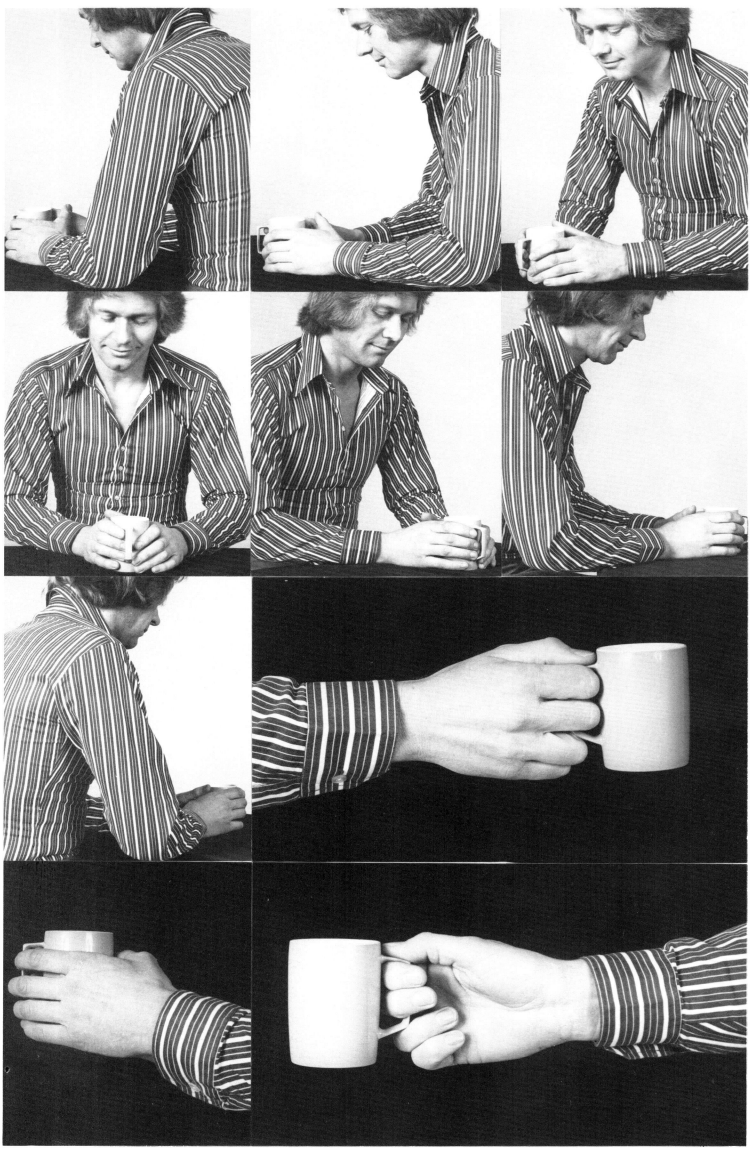

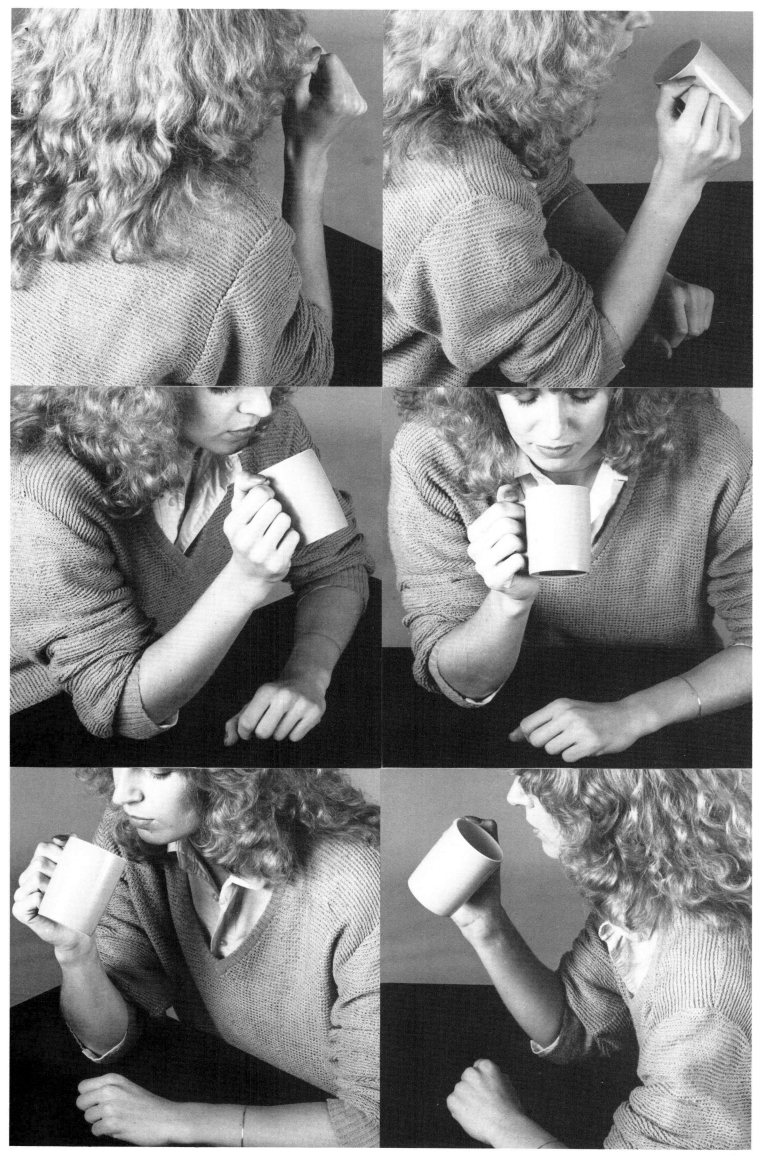

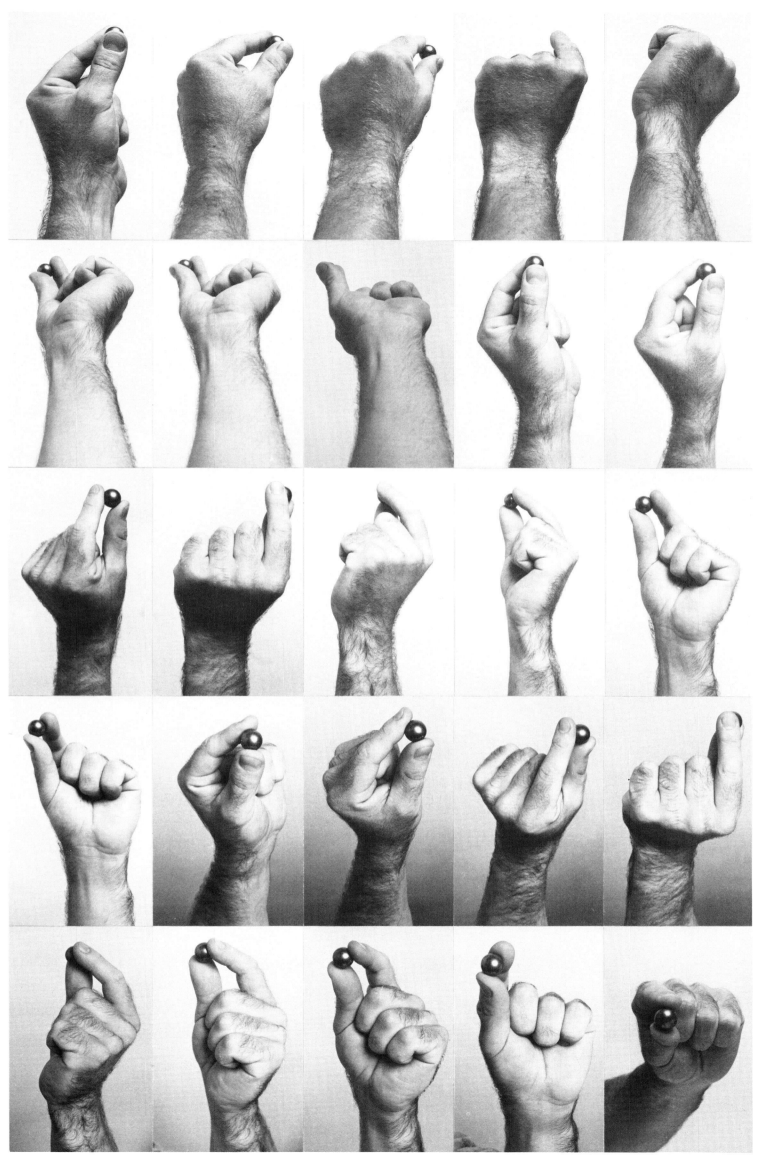

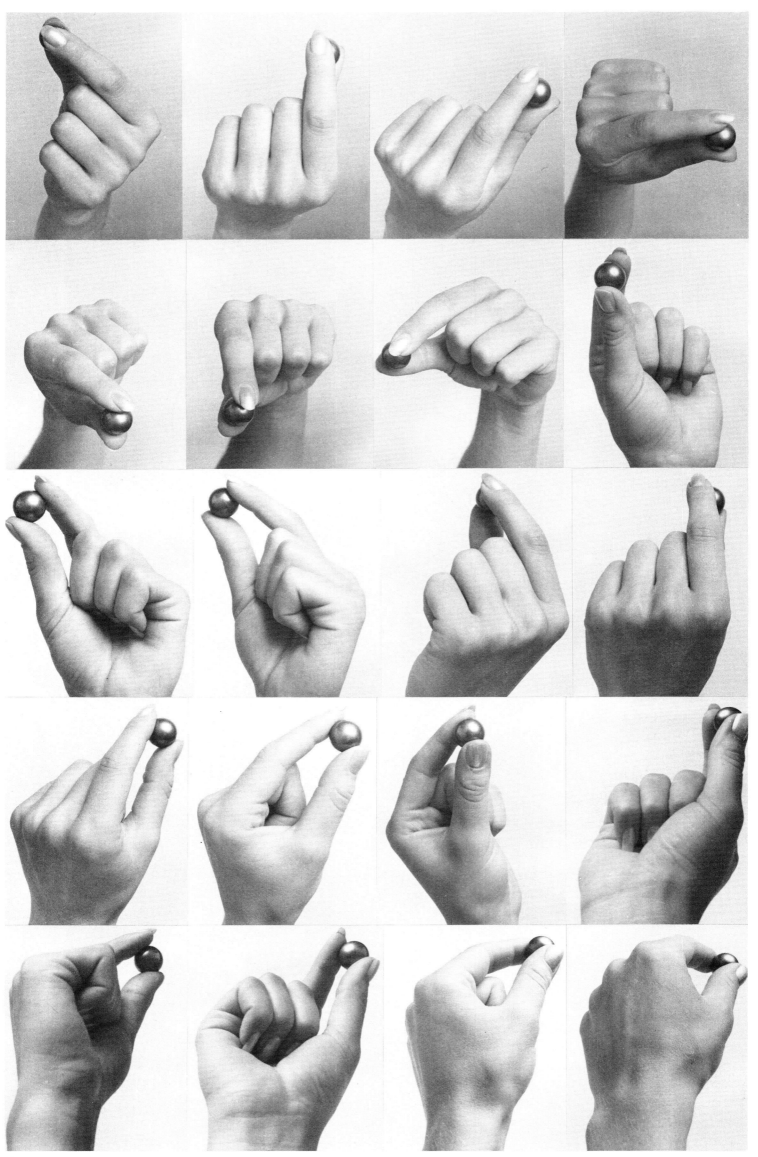

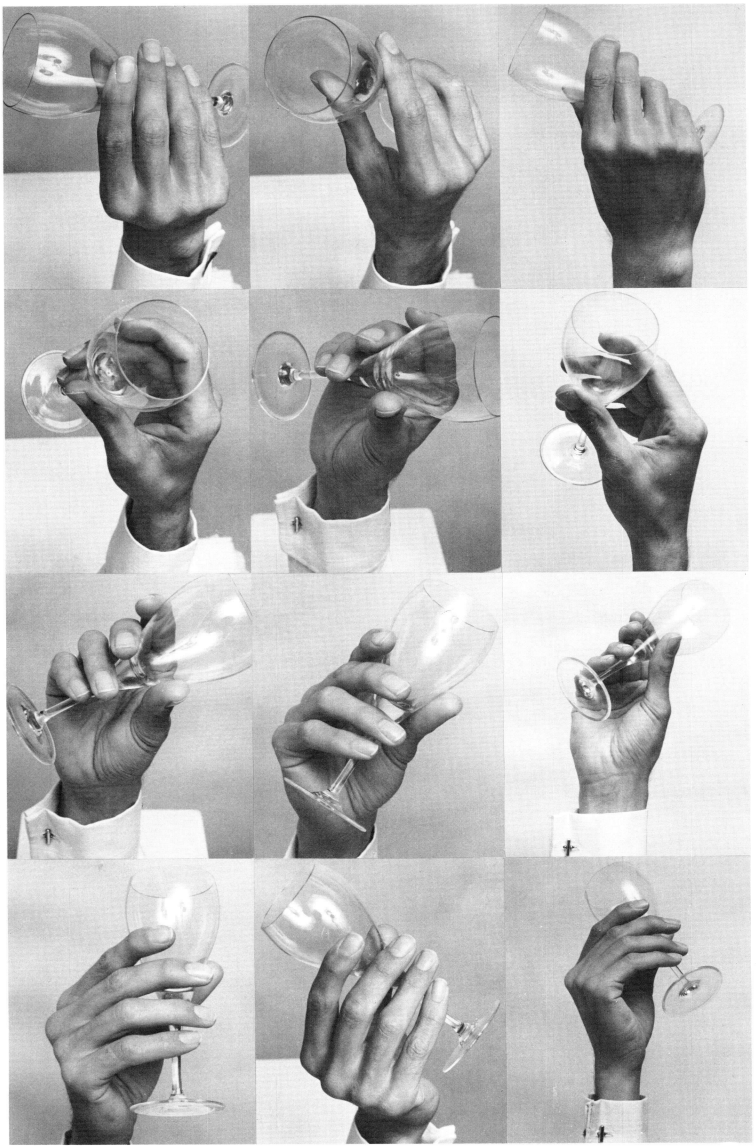

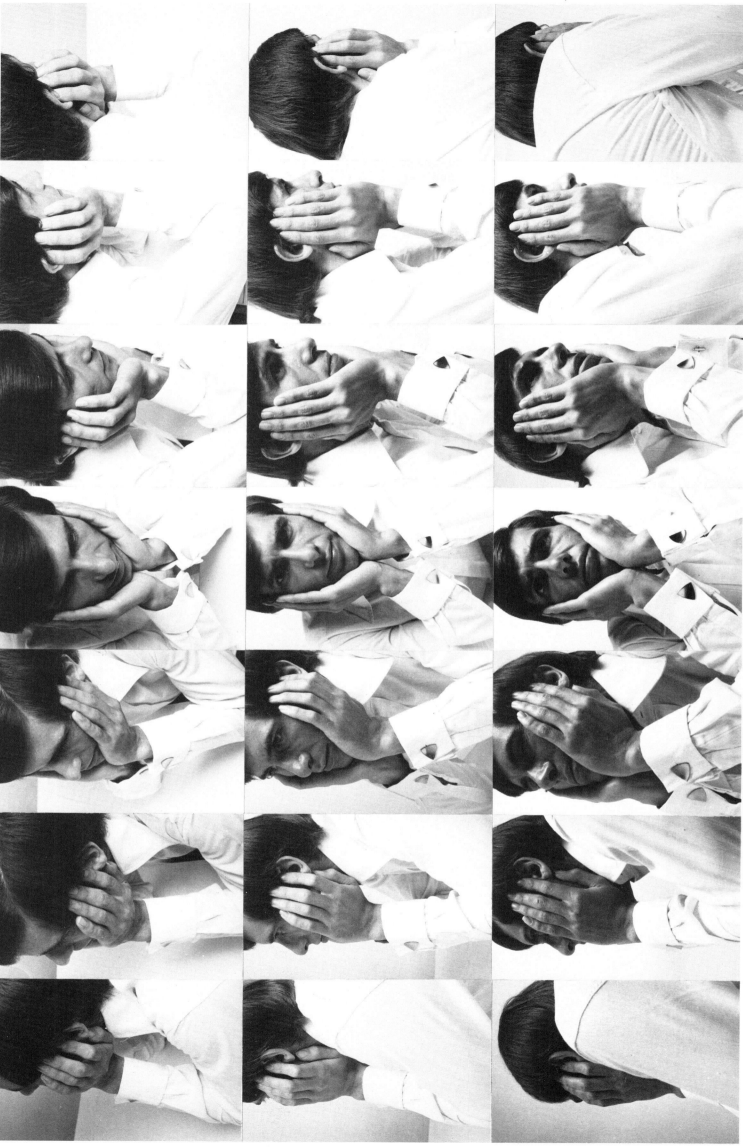

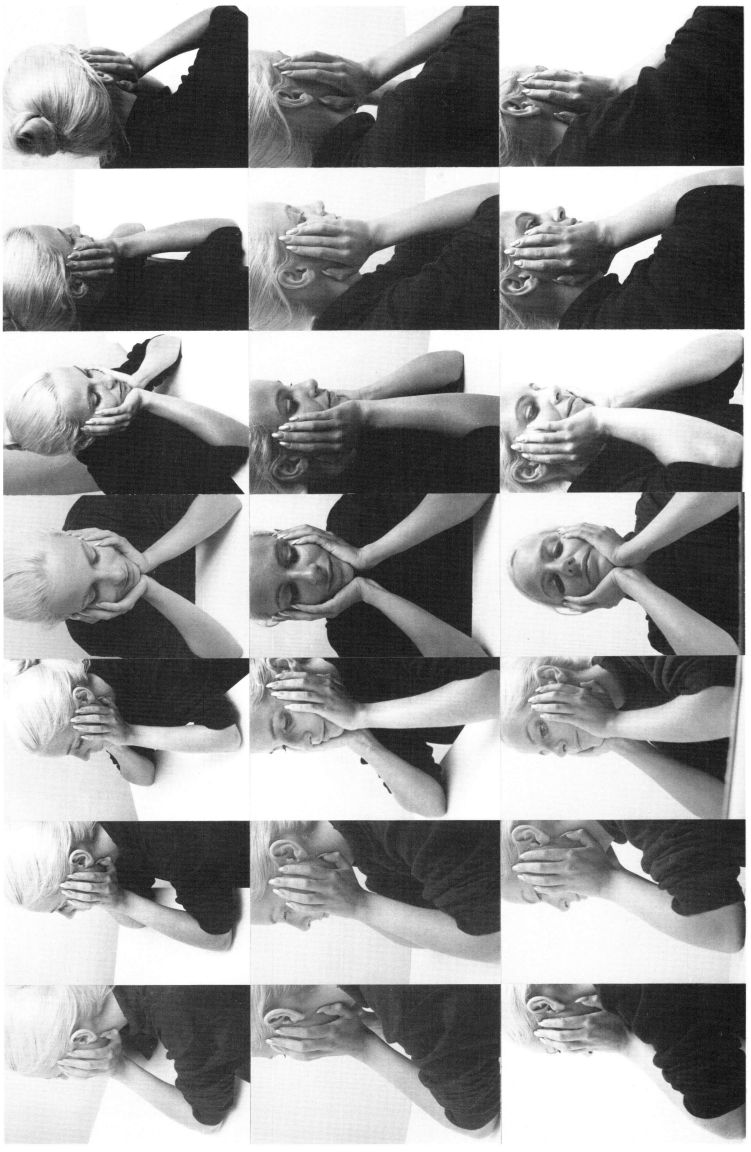

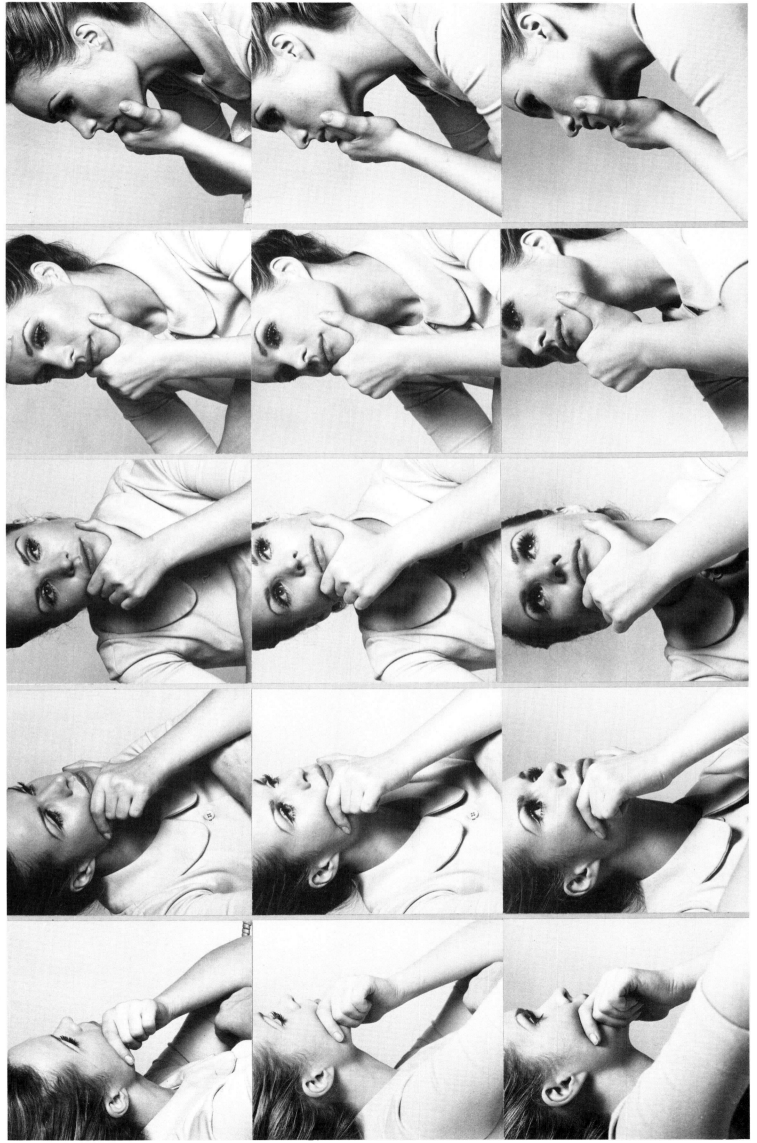

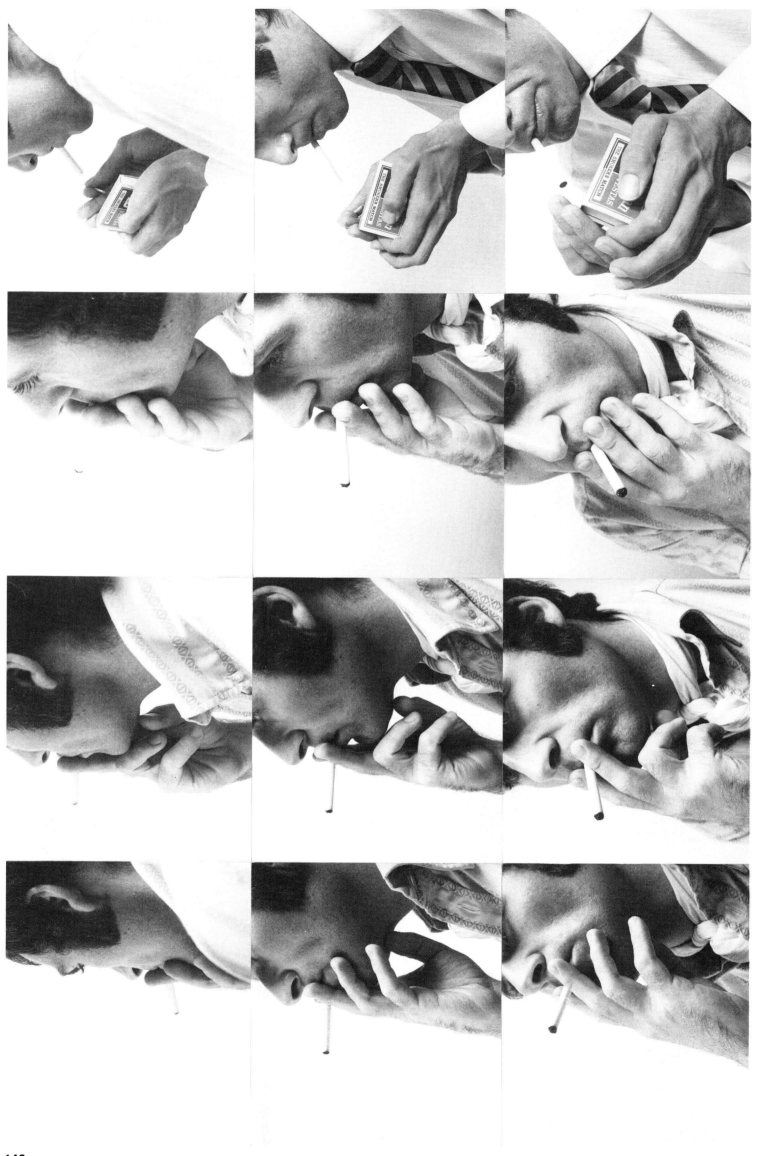

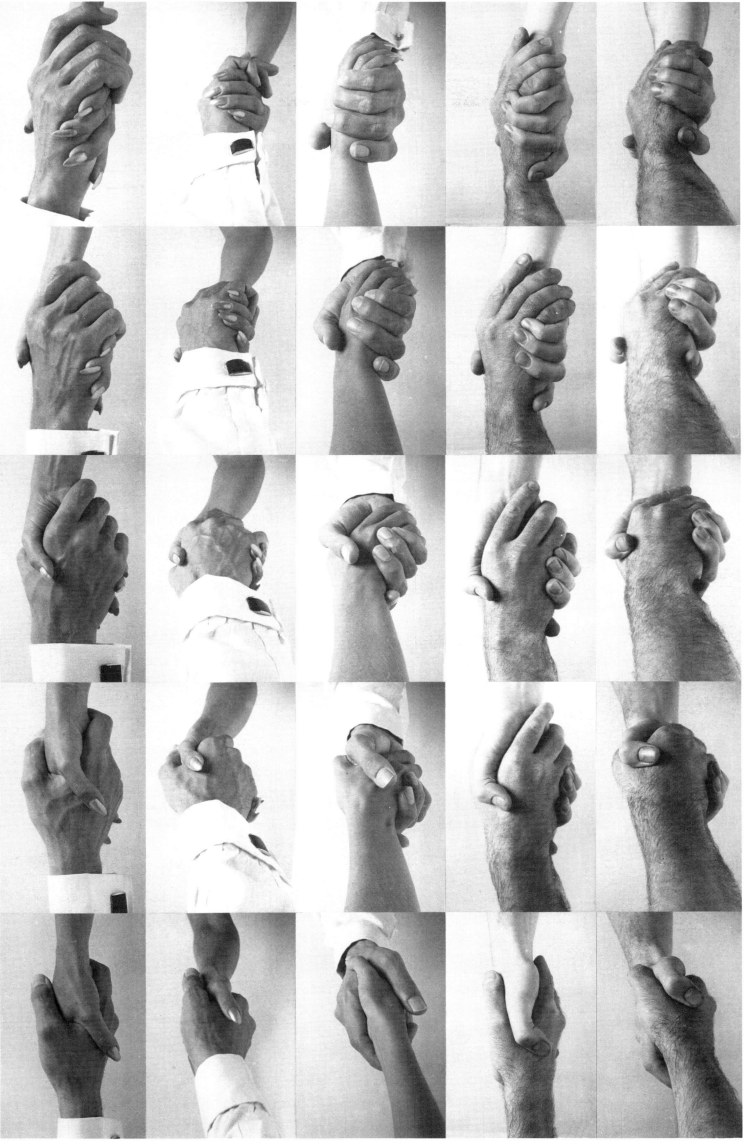

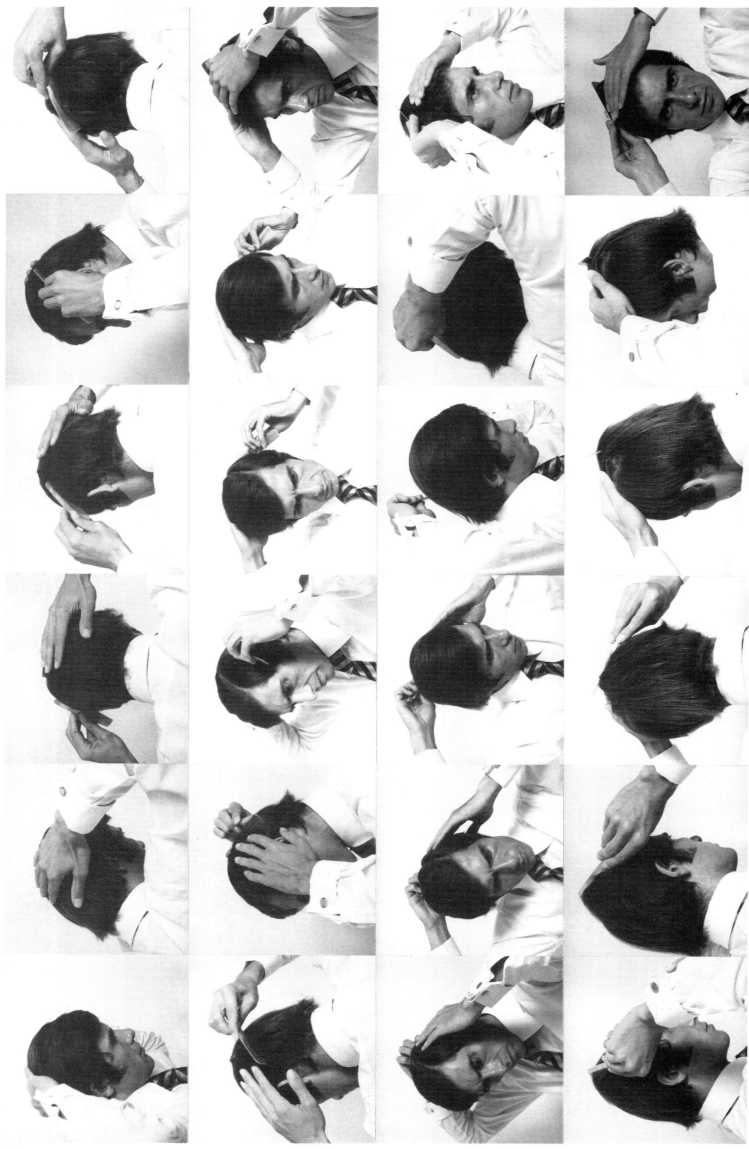

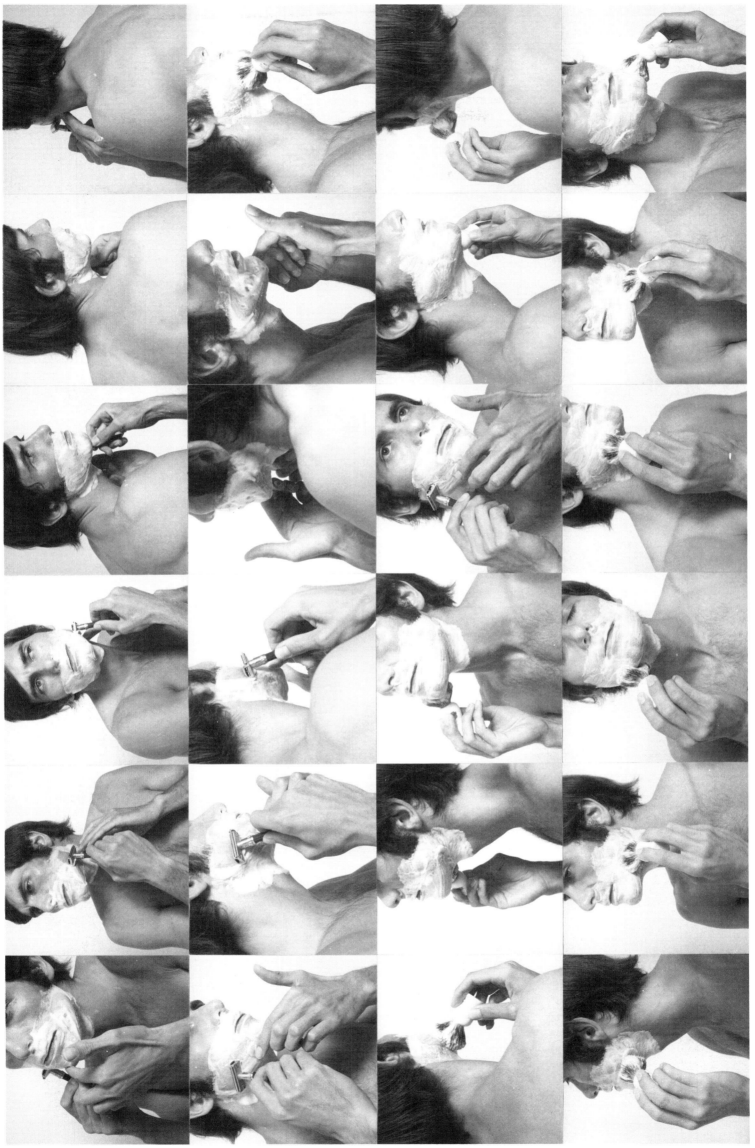

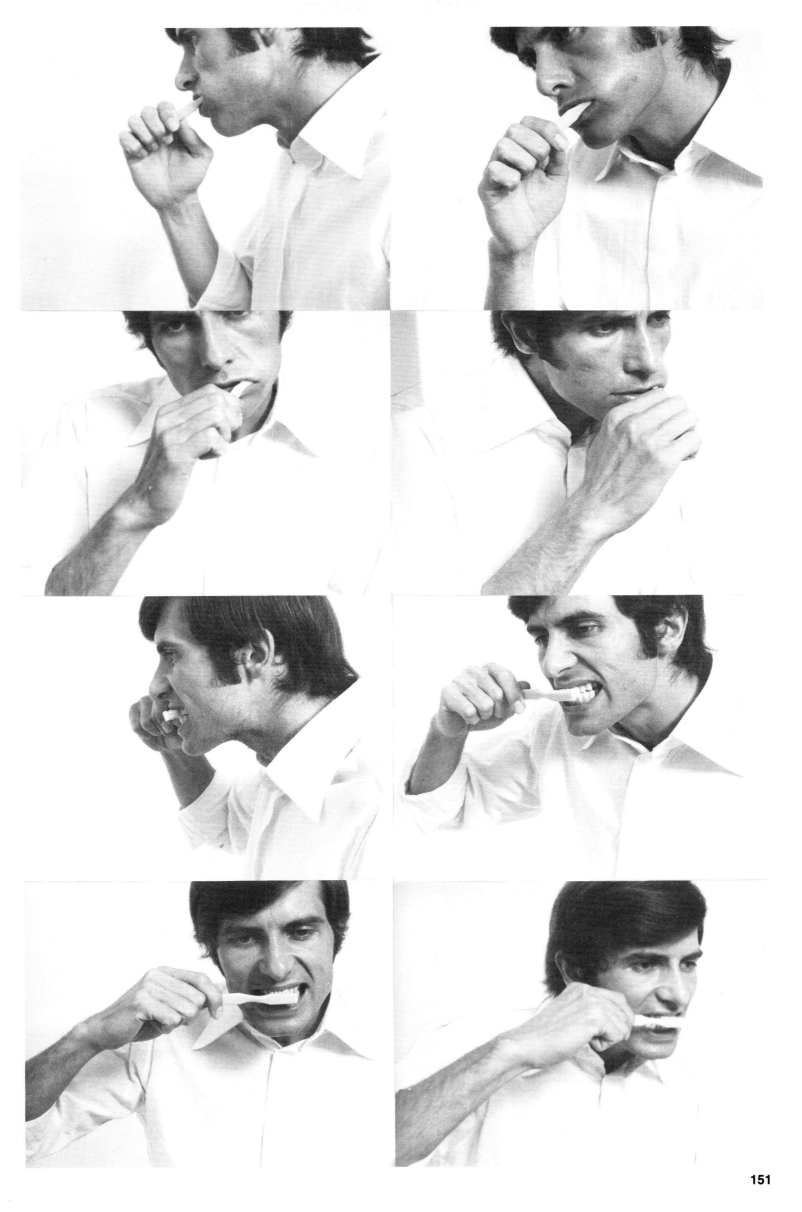

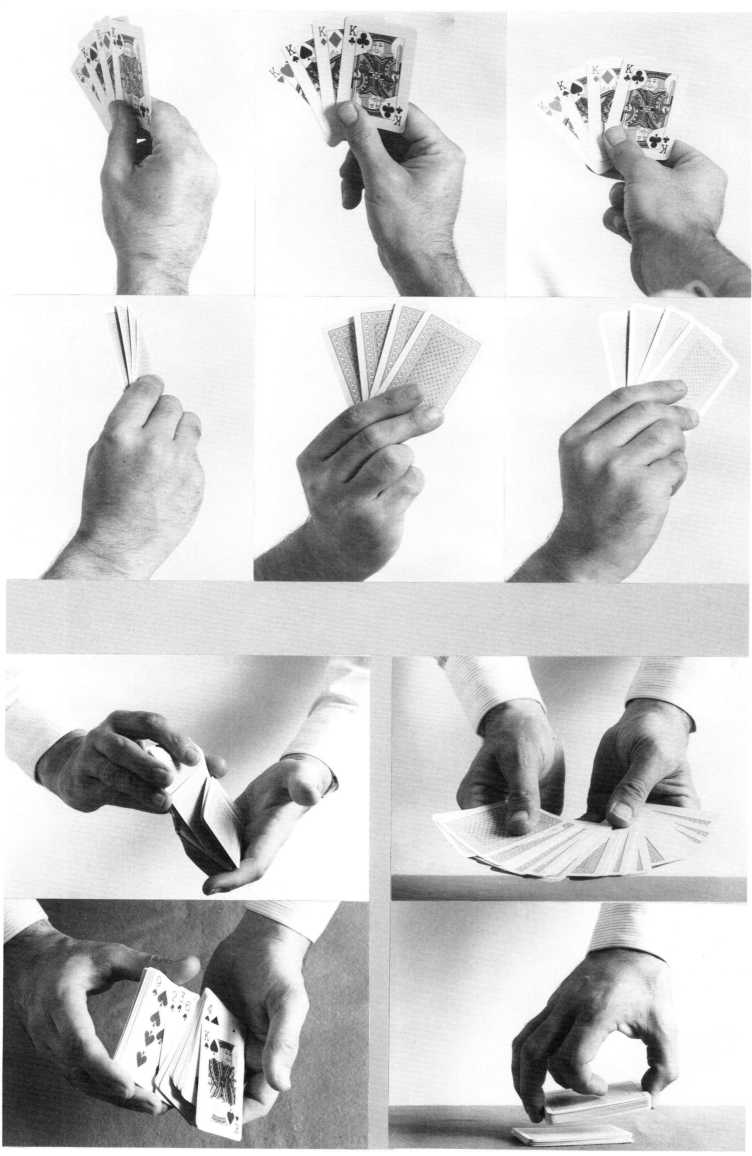

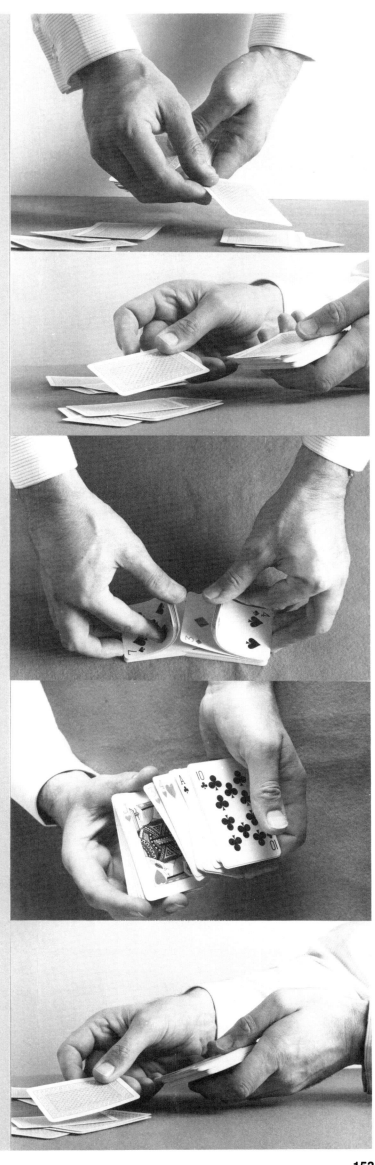

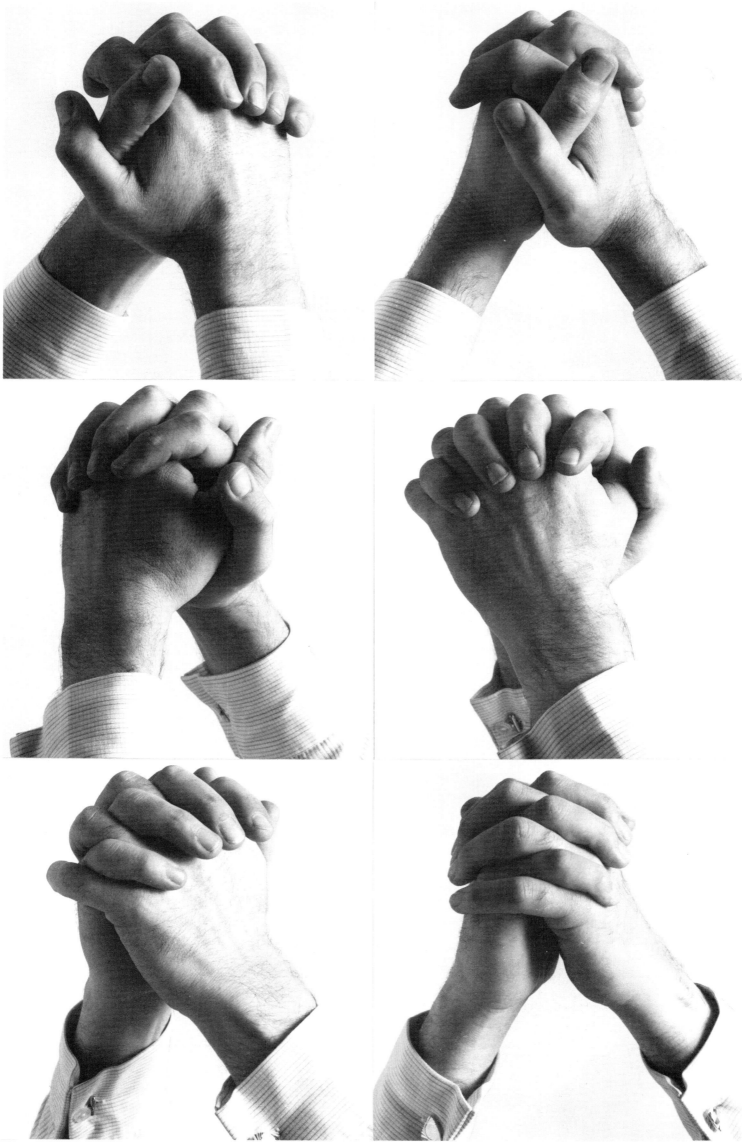

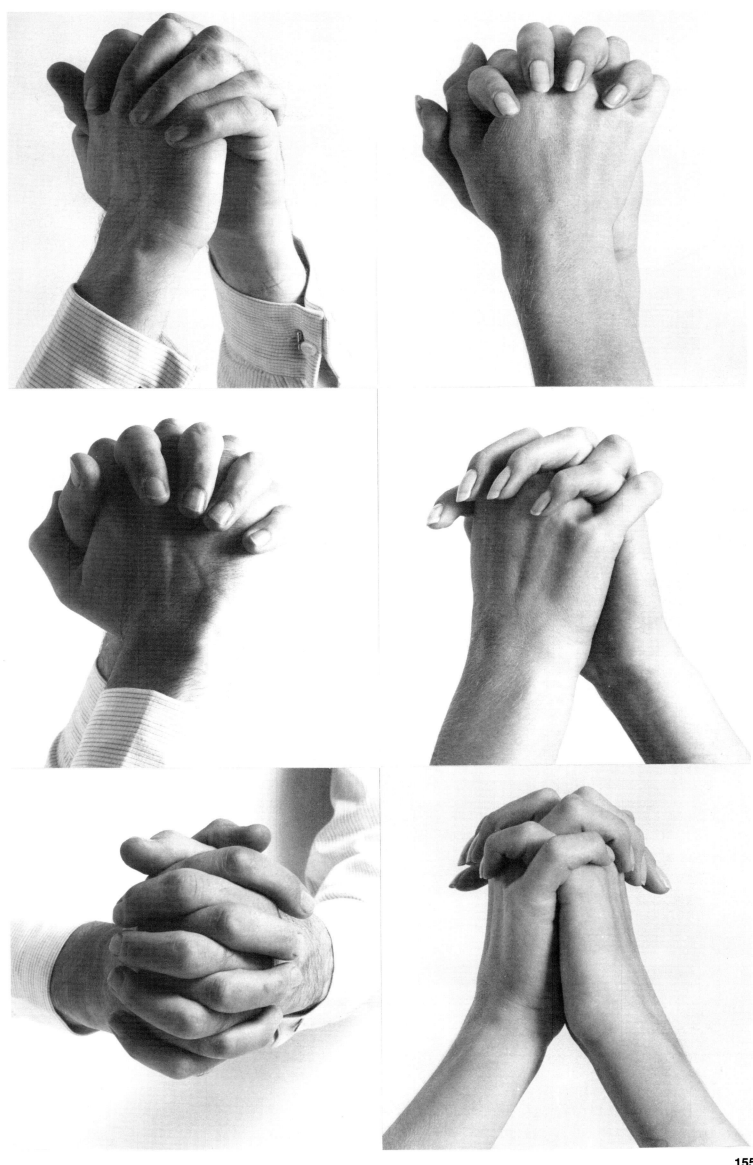

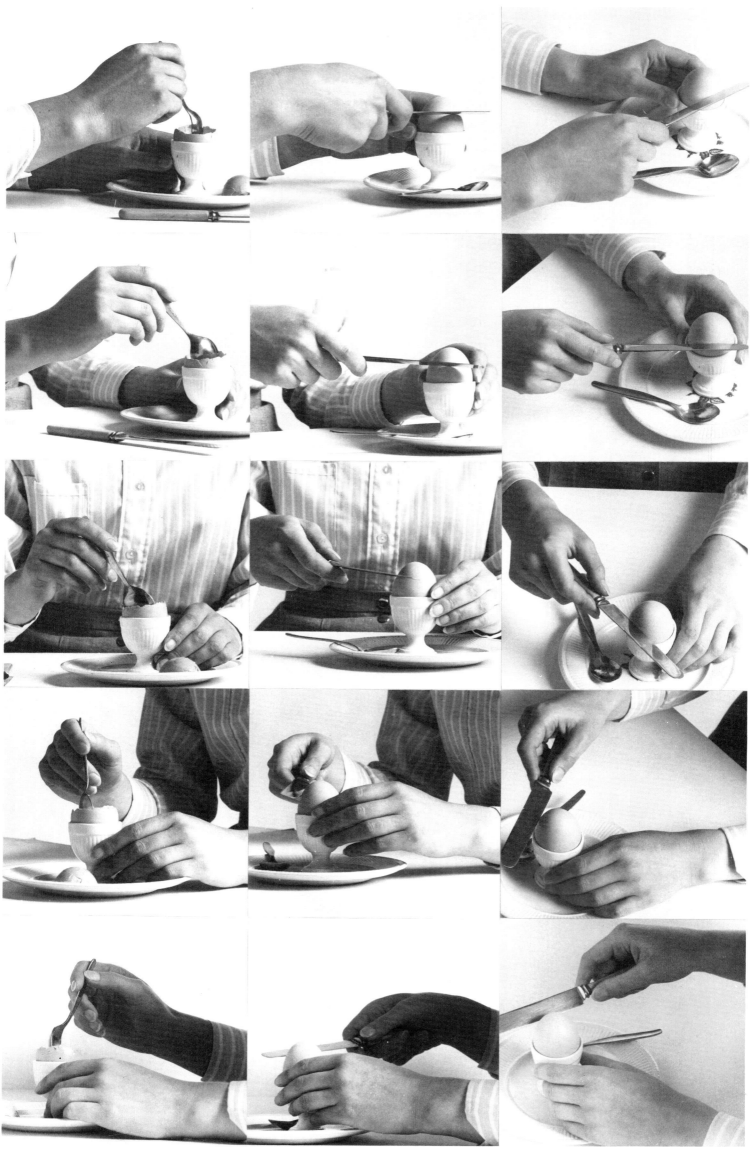

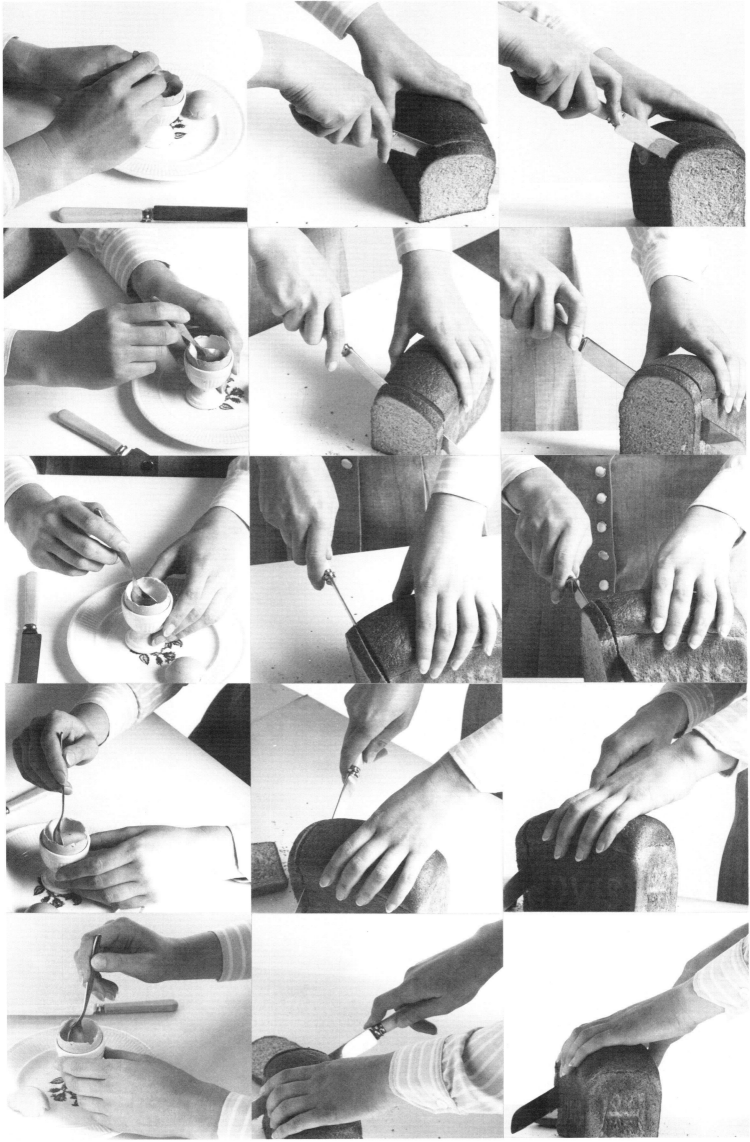

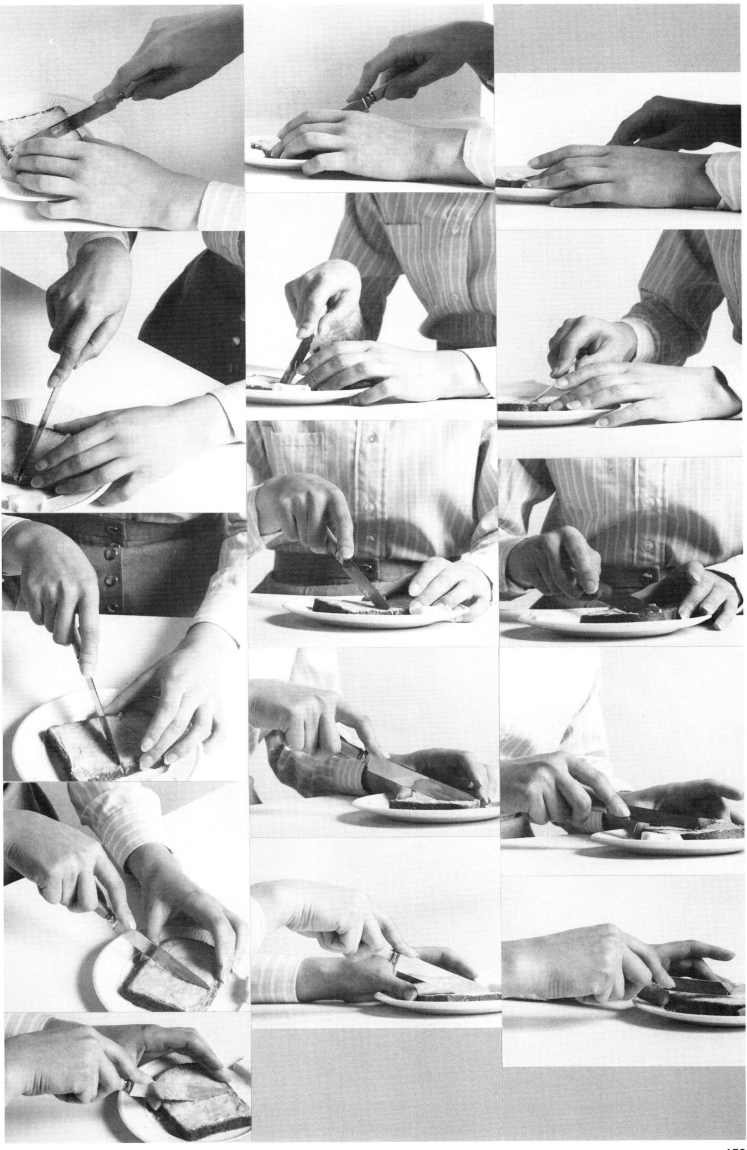